# The Open Gate of Mercy

# The Open Gate of Mercy

Stories from Bangkok's Klong Toey slum

## Fr. Joseph Maier

*Heaven Lake Press*

Distributed in Thailand by:
Asia Document Bureau Ltd.
P.O. Box 1029
Nana Post Office
Bangkok 10112 Thailand
Fax: (662) 260-4578
Web site: http://www.heavenlakepress.com
email: editorial@heavenlakepress.com

First published in Thailand
by Heaven Lake Press
Printed in Thailand

Illustrations: Chingchai Udomcharoenkit © 2012
Jacket design: K. Jiamsomboon
Author's and cover photographs: Yoonki Kim © 2012

ISBN 978-616-7503-14-1

*To our neighbors and friends, How arrogant we are to dare
tell your stories, but humbly we ask your pardon
and forgiveness if we have goofed and not told the story
properly, or showed any disrespect in any way.*

# CONTENTS

## PART III: Children of Klong Toey

## PART IV: Holy Days

**PART V: Father Joe's Notepad**

# Introduction

A young girl wanders in and out of the Pat Pong go-go bars in Bangkok selling flowers to foreigners on holiday. Where did she come from? Who takes care of her? What will become of her?

Four-year-old identical triplet girls are sold for two cases of whiskey. Who buys them? Will they ever go to school? Do they have any chance in life?

A disabled trash-picker stakes her living, along with her hopes and dreams, on her "almost magical" walking cane. Will she make enough today for a few bowls of rice?

Father Joe Maier writes about the poorest of the poor, the people we pass by on the streets, usually without notice, almost invisible. On the surface their daily battles may seem humble and inconsequential, but as Father Joe makes clear in each of the following stories, their battles are no less than epic.

As the Parish Priest for the Catholic community living beside the city's main slaughterhouse and as director and founder of the Human Development Foundation, Father Joe has been walking arm-in-arm with his brothers, sisters, and children in the slums for over 40 years. The stories Father Joe hears and tells are often beyond belief, sometimes rattling our universe and shaking us out of our complacency, though that is surely not Father Joe's intention.

Father Joe is simply expressing his love and respect for the poor, showing us that in spite of a life devoid of privilege, they possess an inner dignity. There's plenty of joy and humor in these stories, too. Only rarely, and only in the most dire circumstances, is there a hint of graveyard cynicism. The slums, Father Joe tells us, are holy places filled with temples, mosques and churches, where weddings, holidays, and festivals take on much greater significance than in the fancier parts of town and where the daily rhythm of life itself is a celebration of love and family.

It may surprise the reader that a 72-year-old slum priest chooses to write in a familiar tone. His stories feel less like set pieces or essays and more like spontaneous conversations between old friends. He writes humbly, from the heart.

One final note: Every person you meet along the way in the following pages has a personal story that is worth passing on. Names, where appropriate, have been changed, nick-names used, and minor details modified. That said, Father Joe is taking you on a journey through the heart of a community that he's devoted most of his life in serving. Many of these stories originally appeared in a slightly different form in the Bangkok Post.

# PART 1

Life Around the Slaughterhouse

# Klong Toey's Granny of the Year

She'll never win the Bangkok Grandmother of the Year award, but she's definitely Granny of the Year in the Klong Toey slum. Yai Sing, or Granny Sing as she's known—and I'll explain that in a minute—rolls her own smokes and earns her own way from her motorcycle-propelled coffee cart. Sports a trademark ancient pair of secondhand twenty-baht (sixty-five-cent) "shades" her granddaughter Mot swapped from a "trader" in a back part of the slum. Two plastic bags of Granny Sing's original blend of ice coffee for the shades.

Seventy-three years old plus some change and, wow, she's out there seven days a week, kick-starting her funky, three-wheeled red motorbike with a cart attached, bouncing through the potholes and rainy season puddles, stopping where she can find some shade to dispense hot and iced coffee, hot and cold sweet tea, Ovaltine and assorted sugary pick-me-ups.

A policeman new to the neighborhood recently stopped her on her motorcycle and asked to see her driving license. "That was fun," she later said. Granny's not fond of policemen on any day of the week, so this was grist for the mill. No, she couldn't complain when they put her daughter, Mot's mom, in prison. Her daughter was a heavy in the

3

drug trade, and fair is fair. But not fair was the rough body search of Mot, her sixteen-year-old granddaughter. Granny hasn't forgotten that.

About twenty of her friends and customers surrounded this policeman and reminded him of the manners that his mama should have taught him. And told him to warn his friends who might also be in uniform to mind their manners. Because this was Granny Sing! That's right.

Grannies play a special role in Thailand. Not that they don't everywhere else, of course, but here in the Kingdom it seems a disproportionate number end up taking care of their grandchildren, after the kids' dads disappear and the mommies go to work or to jail.

Some grannies have been known to put these children to work, selling flower garlands or running drugs or worse. Much worse. That's not Granny Sing. She's the grandmother you read about in storybooks, the one that hardship and tragedy cannot stop. She and her husband came to Klong Toey thirty years ago to work construction at the port. Casual labor. Which means you work when they want you. Minimum wage, no benefits. She gave birth to six children, and the first three died young. Childhood diseases and no real medical care.

Then her husband died. There was some money left over from the neighbors' donations for his cremation. Granny decided that construction work was not for her, and she bought a secondhand bicycle, learned to ride it and began selling iced coffee to support her three youngest. The motorcycle came later, after she'd saved the money for it.

She's been doing this for twenty-six years now, and of the surviving three children two are in jail and the third has disappeared. "He lived in Klong Toey and kept coming around for money," Granny says. "I got tired of throwing him out, so I told the police to come and get him and his drugs. But he skipped town. I hope he doesn't come back for a while."

Of the two in prison, she says only one is worth saving and that's Mot's mom. Mot is with Granny Sing every day, riding pillion on the motorcycle seat, helping mix and serve the coffee. Granny Sing says she won't let the girl out of her sight.

"Mot is sixteen and finished the sixth grade," she says, "and I don't want her married young like I was."

About a year ago Mot said she wanted to paint her grandmother's toenails. Said they'd look good with the worn rubber slippers. Granny Sing said no way, said painted toenails were for sissies and, besides, they wouldn't look good with her type of haircut. She has thick gray hair, cut in a long "military" style.

One day Granny left Mot to look after her coffee cart for a few minutes. She'd heard a favorite old song, a sad Thai love song, on a nearby radio and wanted to dance. So she lifted her arms and turned her hands in the traditional manner, rotating her body slowly, lost for a moment in her memories. There was laughter. Friends called out and joined her, dancing in the street near their ramshackle homes. Good times in the slum.

It turned into a bit of a party. Granny doesn't usually drink, and it was one of those days when there wasn't enough money both to eat breakfast and buy the day's coffee supplies. That left her with an empty stomach, so a couple of shots of moonshine turned the day around for her. That's when Mot painted her granny's toenails. Mot said it looked good, matched the red on the motorbike. But Granny wasn't sorry when the polish wore off.

For the comfort it brings, Granny smokes hand-rolled cigarettes, using local Anchor Brand tobacco called *ya choon*, still sold at five baht in a plastic bag squeezed shut at the top.

She buys it with *bai jak* leaf, two baht a pack with fifty leaves harvested in the swamp and dried. One leaf for a smoke, two leaves if you want a thicker cigarette. For Granny, this is a week's supply.

Sometimes Granny switches to betel nut. Although her coffee-drinking clientele don't mind her smoking, they don't totally approve of the betel, a leaf and areca palm nut and lime paste chew that darkens the gums and teeth and gives the user a slight buzz. They don't mind the habit—many of them chew too—but they fear a bit of her chew might fall into the coffee when she serves it.

Granny Sing generally goes along with this. In fact she's meticulous about the way she runs her coffee cart. She is especially careful about the straws and gives new customers instructions on how to clean them Klong Toey-style. You place the straw in the bag so liquid fills part of the straw; then you place your index finger over the top of the straw, creating a vacuum, and pull the straw out of the bag with the coffee inside; then you turn the straw upside down and release your finger from the end, and the captured coffee runs out onto the ground. In this manner you clean the inside of the straw from any impurities or small bugs that might have made their home there.

Plus, Granny says, you should try to make a bit of "merit" whenever you can each day, and as you release some of the sugared coffee onto the ground, most probably you are giving some hungry ants a bite to eat. To help them make it through the day.

All this for only ten baht! Can those fancy-dancy coffee bars in what are called "better" neighborhoods give you as much for your money?

So let's take it from the top. *Yai* is Thai for grandmother and *sing* is a shortened version of the English verb "to race," as in "ra-cing." Drop the first syllable of "racing," and "Yai racing" becomes Yai Sing. The motorcycle racing granny. Granny Sing. A moniker describing both her own good self and her red motorcycle coffee house.

Last week Granny took nine hundred baht she had saved up and rode the bus up to the Korat Provincial Prison to visit her daughter, Mot's mom. Five hours up, a ten-minute visit, then back again. Tough, if you're seventy-three and some change, to be squeezed into a non-air-con bus. No complaints, though.

The old motorcycle may not kick over every time she puts her slippered foot to the start pedal. But with patience, Granny Sing is on her way. One more plastic bag of ice coffee, one more dream, one more old Thai love song to dance to.

Granny of the Year, Klong Toey-style.

# Klong Toey's Pioneer Amazing Bicycle Breakfast Restaurant

She started her fast-food career selling second breakfasts from her bicycle to "sweat labor" workers in the Klong Toey river port. They'd walk the seven minutes from the riverside docks to a hole they'd knocked in the wall between the port and the slum. Auntie Muey was on the slum side of the wall—safe from nasty Port Authority guards who would want free second breakfasts from her.

And she would sing out her morning menu loudly, at the top of her lungs. It was a rebel song, really, about how "I want to serve you a tasty meal—enough to fill your tummy. Make you men burp! Not cheat you." Every rebel song is truly a love song, and her songs were for the people of Klong Toey.

It began back before container ships and automation. Her husband was a sweat laborer in the holds of ships twenty-three years ago. To keep him strong and to save a few precious baht, she'd cook rice at home and cycle it over to him late in the morning.

Then a neighbor's wife wanted to know if Auntie Muey would cook for her husband too—at half the price of what the vendors charged in the port. So began her rebel songs, shouting out her morning breakfast menu in the Klong Toey slum—and her pioneer Amazing Bicycle Breakfast Restaurant was born.

Auntie Muey is a bicycle-pedaling old-fashioned love story on her two-wheel rig. The bike has an old-style back wheel stanchion for parking when she stops to serve breakfast, lest her Amazing Bicycle Breakfast Restaurant topple over. And it has a platform on the back—like the old bikes that used to double as beasts of burden, carrying hundred-kilogram sacks of rice.

She wears her trademark crisp and clean red apron down to her knees over long, loose, dark Chinese-type trousers, sky blue sneakers and a floppy hat with a flap to shade her neck from the sun. Her size? Medium to small.

Her rig is a full bicycle restaurant serving nine individually wrapped types of rice and chicken, rice and fish, etc. She also has coffee, Klong Toey slum-style, or tea mixed with condensed milk, or her popular red sweet water. And hard-boiled eggs—ten baht for two in a plastic bag, complete with a tiny sack of soy sauce just in case you like your eggs that way. And on some days, delicious freshly fried pork rinds. It's all there on her menu, handwritten daily on a piece of cardboard.

Her rig also carries a polystyrene ice chest on the back. New ice—freshly frozen, she tells everyone, not yesterday's ice refrozen. And she always takes time to listen when a customer, often a friend, feels lonely or sad, or has had a death in the family and would like to sit and chat for a while with Auntie Muey, or simply indulge in the latest Klong Toey gossip for a few minutes while eating breakfast next to her bicycle as the traffic rolls by.

The kids love her. She acts tough, but along her route there are a couple of hungry children living with their grandmother. There's no money, so they usually go to school hungry. But when they hear the ring of her bell they know breakfast is coming. She scolds them, of course! You know the drill—dirty fingernails, hair not properly combed, swearing and so on.

She started her mobile restaurant twenty-three years ago. She's now on her eighth bike, and this one has lasted the longest—ten years. On Buddhist holy days she makes merit by "renting" a small flower lei for five baht and keeping it on her handlebars for blessings and protection during the week.

She's heard of the Catholic Saint Christopher, so she has his medal hanging from the handlebars as well. She says she wants all the heavenly protection she can get.

Over those twenty-three years five of her rigs were stolen. Three times it was at night, and they took just the bicycle from beside her house. The other two times they went after the whole restaurant.

The first time it set her back for weeks. She lost everything—ice chest, plastic drink containers, eight plastic sacks with two hard-boiled eggs each, forty packets of rice and chicken and fish. The whole lot was stolen by drug addicts, but what angered her the most was that they didn't even eat her food, just scattered it along the street.

The second time, a drunk grabbed her restaurant and tried to pedal away, wobbling all over the place. After the first theft, by the drug addicts, her husband had bought her a whistle to blow in case of trouble, but Auntie Muey had tied the whistle on the handlebars of her bike, so she couldn't use it on this occasion. She screamed "Help!" and a neighbor hit the drunk with a broom.

He fell off, and the neighbor grabbed Auntie's restaurant before it crashed. Only the ice chest fell off, spilling the ice. The coffee and the sweet water stayed in the front basket on the bike. They pummeled him thoroughly—he sported big bruises plus a black eye for three weeks. Then he disappeared, and Auntie Muey hasn't seen him since. Everyone said, "Good riddance to bad rubbish!"

Auntie Muey has never taken a spill in her life. But she rides more slowly these days selling her second breakfasts.

Years ago, she'd be singing all morning long. A chant really, calling out her breakfast menu to the ring of her bell. Now it's more the ring of her bell than her singing that you hear. That's since her voice cracked. One chilly morning, maybe seven years ago, she was caught in the rain—soaked to the skin. She had a runny nose and a sore throat and coughed for weeks afterwards.

Her strong singing voice never really came back. So when you see her now and hear the ring of her bell, it seems that your troubles just melt away and you just want to be there. You eat your second breakfast, even though you're not that hungry. You don't know why, really, but your eyes water and you just know she will wipe away all your tears and your pain. Somehow.

She's a Klong Toey pioneer. She invented Klong Toey's first movable restaurant. Maybe the first in Thailand, but we're not too sure about that, so she can't brag too much. But more than anything else, Auntie Muey is a walking, talking old-fashioned food-vending love story.

But in the beginning it wasn't always that way—she didn't always sell food to a grateful public. She began working on building sites at sixteen, unskilled labor in a rural provincial town. Her wages were thirty baht a day. A country girl, she was married and pregnant at twenty-six.

After that there was no more building work as there was no place on a building site for a new mother with a baby. So she had to care for her baby at home in a tin shack. Her husband was a good man. He loved her and gave her his wages. He's still with her, but he's got constant aches and pains from years of lifting and carrying more than he should on his back.

When her baby was five, they moved to Klong Toey. Carrying the baby with her, she took her Bicycle Restaurant along the docks. Then, after nine years, some overzealous guards wearing Port Authority uniforms decided her restaurant was a breach of security.

So she went to work in the shrimp and squid cleaning plant next to the abattoir. But that didn't last. She had to clean the shrimp and squid quickly because the wages were only half a baht to two baht a kilo.

If you moved fast, you could make fifty to seventy baht a day. But to do that, you couldn't wear gloves. The plant's sanitary regulations said you must wear rubber gloves, but with gloves you couldn't work fast enough. You'd make maybe half that and get fired. So you'd work bare-handed. Which was fine, except the brine rotted your fingernails and cuticles.

After seven months her hands were bleeding too much. The factory manager said Auntie Muey was a sanitary risk. So after a month, when her hands had healed, she found her true love—her pioneering, Klong Toey slum-based Amazing Bicycle Breakfast Restaurant.

She's still out there each morning. Come to Klong Toey any time you're looking for a good second breakfast. But come early—she's usually sold out before noon.

# The Flight of the Fruit Bat

A single, rather large, brown-furred, black-winged fruit bat came swooping, screeching out of the sunset sky like it was making a bombing run over the Pai Singto slum on New Ratchadapisek Road. No one had ever seen anything like it.

The slum kindergarten children had seen bats before. They'd been watching a group for over two weeks, ever since the bats had migrated to eat the sweet thorn tree (*ton ngiew*) blossoms. Frightened at first, now the children were fascinated. The Pai Singto school teacher, a wise woman, had decided to make the bats a school project. Soon the children had taken to the bats as their friends, their pets, and could even identify a few of them and had given them names.

The kindergarten at Pai Singto is our smallest. Eighteen children with full attendance. Roughly the same number as the bats. The shack kindergarten is tucked into the far end of the slum, just past the end of the cement walls, open to the sidewalk. The children thus passed the thorn trees each day on their way to and from school.

This slum is one of those long ribbon-type slums you see all over Bangkok, extreme poverty providing sad contrast to the rest of the neighborhood. With the huge Convention Center and the Stock Exchange of Thailand across the street, and a multi-storey office complex just down the street, perhaps nowhere else in the city is there greater disparity. The people are poor, most selling fruit daily from pushcarts and sidewalk noodle shops.

Slums are fragile, and Pai Singto is more fragile than most. Just thirteen meters wide and over four hundred meters long, its 125 scrap wood, metal-roofed shacks are hidden by three-meter-high concrete walls on each side. So when the sunset fire began, soon after the male bat swept past, it was like an inferno in a wind tunnel, and in a flash fifty-four homes were gone. The fire stopped a few meters short of our shack kindergarten facing the sidewalk, just beyond the walls.

Most slum fires are caused by negligence, and this one was as well, but grannies told the children a bit of the "lore of old," that the fire was because of what happened to the bats. In their yearly migration the bats had come to dine on the sweet flowers of the two big thorn trees near the wall, then hung from the trees as bats do, resting up before feasting again. For two weeks they had eaten peacefully. People who know of such things say these bats only come to serene places and bring good fortune—when they are treated properly. By now, as a class project, the school children had all drawn pictures of their favorite bat, tree and flowers.

That was before Mr. Sanop, a nasty old piece of work who lived in the slum, began taking potshots at the bats with a slingshot. Three kindergarten children saw him and told their grannies, but grannies and five-year-olds simply do not have the "fire power" to combat a nasty.

The thorn tree is so called for the hundreds of needle-sharp bumps that grow around the trunk. Some people call it the "hell tree" because if you're a certain kind of sinner, guilty of sexual crimes, you must spend long years climbing up and down the tree, as your flesh is torn to pieces. And if you were especially hurtful, crows come and peck at your exposed bottom for added insult. Someone wistfully asked, "Does this particular punishment also include those who hurt bats?"

But it's also considered a tree that brings good fortune. An older slum lady appointed herself as our trees' keeper and protector. For a small fee, she allowed folks to come and scrape the trees with a dull knife, making a paste of flour and water to bring out any lottery numbers that might be inscribed by nature—or the spirits—on the smooth green trunk between the bumps.

Mr. Sanop wasn't much of a marksman, even when sober, but after a while he hit one of the bats, a female. Broke her wing. She hung on for almost two days, with the broken wing moving limply in the breeze. He tried to find someone to wager how long it would take the bat to fall. Finally, the animal weakened and dropped onto the corrugated tin roof of the shack below. The man who lived there retrieved the bat and stuck it, still alive, in an old cardboard box. By this time, the children knew and wanted to feed sweet blossoms to the wounded bat, but the man cursed them.

Then someone in the man's circle said, "Hey, you can eat bat! Cook it up like field rat or cobra. It's good for you. Makes you strong. Cook it up spicy, wash it down with whiskey."

The sidewalk noodle shop by the gate leading into the slum was a favorite for the area's tuk-tuk drivers, and when one of them heard about the bat, he agreed that he'd kill and skin it. The children in school next door overheard the whiskey talk and were horrified. They told their teacher, but she was too frightened to say anything. They killed the bat about noon. Cooked it up about three.

Now here is where the story mixes fact and myth. Some eyewitnesses say that when they gutted the bat, they found it was a pregnant female. Other eyewitnesses say the bat was not pregnant. And you know, of course, that bats do nurse their young. But at least the nasties had the decency not to let the children watch. Or maybe they were ashamed.

They got really into the drinking around four. An hour after that, the large male bat arrived, making three oblong flights over the slum, from one end to the other and back again, screeching loudly. The fire started about six, as the sun went down. It began at one end of the slum next to a furniture factory, where Grandpa Boonmee had built a small fire to boil some water. Once he had the kindling aflame, he wandered away for just a moment to buy a ten-baht shot of Siang Chun whiskey, the local favorite of folks that age.

Mr. Boonmee had helped us build our kindergarten twenty-one years ago. He is eighty-six years old and has been a bag man or rag man for much of his life, salvaging scrap metal and plastic and paper in his cart from the neighborhoods nearby. His day's collection—the plastic bags he'd washed in a canal, the paper he'd dried in the sun—caught fire. His lean-to home was next to the furniture factory, and by the time he returned after drinking his whiskey, both structures were aflame.

The fire started away from where the thorn trees stood and where the bat was killed and eaten. The wind changed and swept back as the fire burned house by house. Poisonous snakes and rats and other creepy-crawlies that lived under the houses tried to escape along with the residents, who were carrying whatever they could grab.

The fire engines came, but before you can use the water hoses, you have to shut off the main electrical grid for the area. You can't douse live electric wires. The 220 voltage runs right up the stream of water and can electrocute the fireman. So in such fires, by the time the Metropolitan Electricity Authority gets the word to cut the power, it's usually far too late. Besides, if you don't put out a slum fire in the first few minutes, the fire goes out of control, as gas cylinders used for cooking explode and spin like pinwheels or shoot like rockets, torching the flimsy wooden homes as if someone had taken a flamethrower to them.

Watching the fire, one of our third-year kindergarten boys went berserk. Screaming, running back into the flames to tell the fire not to hurt his granny's house. His granny couldn't hold him. He wiggled loose and a slum girl, just getting on a motorcycle with her pimp to go to work, rushed over and grabbed him, and together they cried and cried like the world had come to an end. And that day, that minute, for that six-year-old and the bargirl ... it had.

One after another in rapid succession, the houses were destroyed, falling in on themselves, until the flames reached the house where the bat eater lived. His was the last to go. Then the fire stopped. The children all agreed that the flight path of the bat was almost exactly the path of the fire.

The grannies said that the screeching had been the male bat searching for his mate. Chewing betel nut, they solemnly pronounced to everyone who would listen: "The fire knew. The bat told the fire where to burn!" The slum dwellers said the bats had not cursed them, but that they, the people, had brought the curse of the fire upon themselves.

A few days after the smoke and reek of the fire had gone, a handful of the older, more pious residents gathered in front of the thorn trees, which somehow the blaze had missed. They believed they had to make atonement to the guardian spirits of the place and to the bats and to the trees, lest something worse befall them. The children attended also. They had drawn new pictures of the bats.

In Thai it's called the *khaw khama la tode* ceremony. It is done traditionally with nine joss sticks, the head of a pig and an open bottle of twenty-eight-degree whiskey, or even the stronger forty-degree, with a bit poured into a glass. One by one the men and women prayed, "I am from this Pai Singto slum and here to ask pardon for what has happened."

Two days after the ceremony was completed, the other bats returned to the thorn trees and resumed eating the remaining sweet flowers. And then they migrated on.

Today, almost two months later, the houses are being rebuilt. Grandpa Boonmee, at the strong suggestion of police, has moved in with his daughter so as not to be left to boil water on his own. Mr. Sanop, the man with the slingshot, still lives in the slum but is an outcast. The guy in the shack where the bat fell is shunned by the community. The tuk-tuk driver doesn't come to eat noodles at the sidewalk shop any more. The man who ate the bat—who says he might eat bats again, "depending on how hungry I am"—was put to work rebuilding the burned homes. The whiskey group still drink in late afternoons, but even the shadow of a bat flying over them drives them to the thorn trees to light a joss stick.

In addition to their own ceremonies the community asked the monks to bless their new houses—to petition the guardian angels, the spirits of the place, not to be angry, so that the future of the slum would be safe. Most of the community attended the chanting of the holy sutras.

The parents asked if I would re-bless our small kindergarten. They asked me also if Catholics have a special blessing for bats. So I looked in the old Latin Rituale. There is a blessing for school buildings, but for bats ... What we do have is a blessing for flying creatures, large and small. I thought that would suffice.

A few of the children have now convinced their parents to buy them Batman costumes, and these children wear them to school. They hope the bats will return next year. Also the braver ones wear their costumes in front of Mr. Sanop's shack, taunting him and then running away in glee.

All this was told to us by Uncle Mawn, a respectable man who is sixty years old, and Mrs. Jampee, who have lived in the Pai Singto slum for years and years.

Was there a connection between the killing of the female bat and the fire? You decide. I'm just retelling the story.

# Heaven's Door Opened on Soi Cowboy

Years ago now, maybe eleven, his granny died just after a terrible slum fire. That horrible night, teenager Gee carried her out of their shack and watched it burn.

Then Gee met another granny, not his precisely, but she would become his. You'll see. Miss Wandee, in her full-length white cotton dress, is so beautiful with her long black hair sprinkled with the tiniest bit of gray. Gee says that tiniest sprinkling makes him love her more—makes her more special than any of the other girls on the street. And most certainly those around the Portable Four-Wheel Whiskey Bar next to Soi Cowboy.

For all her thirty-six years on the planet, Miss Wandee's been looking for someone to truly love her and offer her whole life to—every breath, every beat of her heart, every blink of her eyes. She's one of those all-or-nothing girls. And she's found roustabout young master Gee.

She'd started her teen years gullible, not cool. Had her first child at sixteen. The father? A Bangkok jock, visiting relatives. Sweet promises, but never returned. The second time it happened, eight years later, was worse. Her momma said, "Girl, you should have known better."

Anyway, her angels were with her. She somehow escaped the Fatal Virus, as did her second baby daughter. But the man

20

... well, he's dead now. AIDS. Gone on to heaven, as they say. Miss Wandee and baby are healthy. Luck of the draw.

But Miss Wandee hooking up with roustabout young master Gee? In a word—brilliant!

Her two daughters, the oldest with a child of her own, accept Gee. But really, in blunt language, twenty-four-year-old Gee married a grandmother—a young granny, but still a granny. A thirty-six-year-old country girl with long black hair with a sprinkling of gray officially marrying twenty-four-year-old street kid Gee—that was a huge leap that only love could make.

Miss Wandee came to the Portable Four-Wheel Whiskey Bar in Soi Cowboy from a town in the province of Uttaradit by way of the island of Samui in the middle of southern Thailand. A five-year journey.

In the provincial town, times were desperate, impossible. Not enough money from the greens she and her momma were hawking by the railway tracks. A girlfriend invited her to Samui. Always room for one more girl at the bar. After a bit of sweat and tears, Miss Wandee became a part-time cashier at the bar. But one midnight she had to run, not because she'd cheated—she hadn't—but because the owner wouldn't keep his hands off her. His "live-in" was not pleased. Laid a loaded pistol on the bar counter next to the cash box. No words were said.

Miss Wandee, as she tells the story, didn't panic. She just took her purse from behind the cash box and walked out of the bar. Didn't look back. Didn't even go back to her rented room for her clothes. Went to the pier to wait for the morning ferry from the island to the mainland, enough money with her for the ferry and a bus to Bangkok. She knew a girl working in Soi Cowboy. Got there, hung around a few days, and by luck the Portable Four-Wheel Whiskey Bar needed an honest cashier.

There is much more to say about both Gee and Miss Wandee. Teenage Gee playing lead guitar and singing vocals in his Baby Ghost Slum Band and the two gigs they played before he went back to reform school. His kicking a year-long glue sniffing habit. Selling flowers on street corners. Becoming a monk for three months.

Miss Wandee was top in her class in grade school, but there was no money to continue. She was always good in arithmetic, counting change for her momma since she was six years old, so her momma didn't get cheated. There was the time the big python snake ate the neighbor's cat, but that story and others are for another day.

Now they've told us that Miss Wandee is going to have another baby. Gee wants to make sure they have the name chosen before she goes to the hospital. When Gee was born, he was given the generic hospital name of Kwan—a name for babies who are abandoned, born to moms without proper documents or with no dad in sight. Miss Wandee is happy. Wants to go home to Uttaradit to give birth because all her family is there to help her care for the new baby.

Gee will be twenty-five soon, a full mature adult. He wants to play his guitar and sing his song "Knock, Knock, Knocking on Heaven's Door" the day their baby is born, so that his granny will look down from the stars in heaven and bless them specially.

They lost everything in the fire. Even Granny's antique betel nut chewing box. With no home, living "makeshift" on the street, Granny died only two days later. For roustabout young master Gee, she was his only family.

He'd dropped out of school and grown up mostly alone in the slums and alleyways of Klong Toey. He spent some time with us here at the Mercy Centre, where he went to school for a while.

Over the next eleven years he became a "kid fixture" around the bars and pubs of Soi Cowboy—loved by "aunts," girls and cops. Gee the survivor was always ready to run an errand, to help out. Everyone tried to take care of him as best they could, street-bar-style, especially some good and kind policemen who saw him more like a son and not a thug or even a street kid. So they tried to protect him too. Of course the law is the law, but everyone knew that their secrets were safe with Gee.

Now he works at the Portable Four-Wheel Whiskey Bar on the sidewalk next to Soi Cowboy. Each evening at eight o'clock he pushes in the portable bar from its daytime storage place and gets it ready for business.

One night at the portable bar Gee met his future *gik* (friend who is more than friend) and bride, Miss Wandee, a fine woman with a face of "beauty beyond," willowy and tall as Gee—and with that lovely gray-sprinkled hair. She had come to be the cashier at the Portable Four-Wheel Whiskey Bar.

His job is to get everything ready. He does the physical stuff, like get the ice and set up the four bar stools. Miss Wandee does the girl part—keeps the whiskey glasses shiny and clean, stocks the paper napkins and takes the money.

Then at three o'clock in the morning, when everyone is going home, Miss Wandee counts the cash, balances the books, cleans the whiskey glasses, counts the bottles of soft drinks sold, etc., while Gee closes down the bar. He drains the ice, stacks the four stools properly and pushes the bar back to the storage area. The sidewalk must be clear by dawn so as not to bother the daytime folks, who mostly don't want a drink of whiskey before they go to work.

Part of roustabout young Gee's job at Soi Cowboy is to stick around until closing time. Just in case. During the midnight hours he plays his guitar and sings if any customers want to listen. His repertoire consists of five Thai songs and two in English. It brings tears to your eyes when he sings "Knocking on Heaven's Door." He has most of the words down. Says he played it nightly for his granny.

At first Miss Wandee paid him no mind. But during the slow times at the bar, when there weren't many customers, they would chat. Slowly they became acquainted. She asked him why he sang that song "Knocking on Heaven's Door" each evening. So he told her about his granny.

Granny loved him in her whiskey-drunk sort of way. Actually stopped drinking booze for him. The abrupt stopping gave her the DTs—trembling madness, shaking for weeks on end. That's unbelievable love. So that Young Gee could eat, at least most of the time, as there simply wasn't enough money. Also she put him into school, even though she never had the chance to go herself. True, he began a couple of years late, but he remembers Granny saying, "Son, it's the learning that counts. How you finish, not when you start."

Over the months Gee and Miss Wandee fell in love. Gee saved his money and one night before singing his song, he told Miss Wandee he'd like to dedicate it to her also. Would she be offended? She was pleased, and after the song, he asked her to marry him. She said yes, and soon after they traveled the eight hours by train to the town in Uttaradit province. She took him home to meet her mother.

Miss Wandee—her teeth not exactly perfect, but blessed with surpassing beauty—had grown up with her momma. They were barely able to make ends meet by selling the green vegetables they grew on their farm to third-class passengers on the morning train through the open windows. The train stops for six or seven minutes in Uttaradit before going on to Bangkok, eight hours away.

Two daughters to her name Miss Wandee had never had a proper wedding but now at thirty-six going thirty-seven Miss Wandee was a blushing bride. On that day in Uttaradit the beautiful granny was a proper bride. You know, in an old-fashioned wedding. Early morning making-merit to the monks. The groom's procession leading to the bride's house, where her parents accept the groom. Proper seating of the elders, and the groom coming to sit next to his bride. The ritual counting of the dowry money and examining the gold neck chain, plus the proper foods in both the procession and the wedding ritual. The approval and blessing of the elders.

All that being completed, then there was food and drink all afternoon and into the early evening. The sleeping room for bride and groom was prepared with flowers. And as always, sometime during the meal, one of the eldest of the ladies present—after a wee swallow of amber liquid for the sake of courage—crooned love songs of long ago, remembering her own wedding day.

# The Anonymous Fate of Miss Na

Her nickname was Miss Na. She had to think twice to remember her given name, written down in some official ledger or computer somewhere. Everyone called her Na.

Na was the oldest daughter in a street family. She and her family actually lived under a grove of sacred trees here in Klong Toey, in the crudest of shelters. There's maybe—if you'd buy it new from the store—two hundred baht's worth of material, in total, in their three shacks. That's about six or seven US dollars' worth. No electricity of course. Water is bought, for five baht a bucket, from a slum lady about one hundred meters away and then hand-carried. They make their living as scavengers, but nowadays, with our economic boom, you see lots of folks scavenging. The competition is fierce.

And of course their lives are at the mercy of the whims of the going-bald fat lady who buys their scavenged goods. She doesn't ask questions about anything they bring, but naturally there's a price attached to her silence, isn't there? You get a better price down the street, but down there, there are always questions. Take your choice.

But the fat lady doesn't like Na's family very much. Her favorite junkyard dog simply got up one day about a year ago and followed Miss Na home to the grove. Wouldn't leave her. He followed Miss Na everywhere, protected her till she went to prison, and now, ever since she died, he howls at the full moon.

Miss Na's family has lived in the grove several years now. They feel safe there. Feel that the spirits of the place protect them. The trees are old. We're not sure, but they were probably planted over fifty years ago around an original temple here in Klong Toey. With the development of the port, the authorities had moved the whole temple to a more viable, accessible location, next to a main road and out of the middle of the port area, because it had not seemed proper to have a holy place in the commercial setting. But no one had dug up the trees and they have flourished there for fifty years. They're special trees, the type you plant around a temple. And that's where Miss Na and her family moved after a slum fire some years ago.

She died in prison, almost—finally ending up in the hospital. She was twenty-three years old. She was innocent. She did not use drugs, she didn't peddle drugs. She hated drugs, but she had been sitting there under the trees when the police came. The whole place had reeked of glue. The men in her clan sniffed glue when they could afford it as it's usually cheaper than booze.

With them, she got grabbed in the dragnet. Accomplice. For the police that word looks good in the records—the more you catch, the more rewards. That junkyard dog bit one of them when they made a move toward Miss Na. She ran in panic and they chased her down. That's when the dog bit the policeman. That made him angry, and maybe that's why they arrested Miss Na too.

She shouldn't have run. They can do anything they want, you know. Everyone said she was clean.

So she spent three hard years in women's prison and was going on four. I say "hard" because she had no money to

27

buy what she needed inside and to protect herself from the predators.

"Almost" dying in prison means that three days before she died of AIDS, she was finally shipped to a hospital near there. It's not good for prison records if there are too many deaths during any particular year. Goofs up the statistics.

So she died in a hospital nearby. There's a really good team of social workers there, folks who care. They didn't know her but stayed with her, holding her hand when she died. It helped when they told her mom that her daughter hadn't died alone. Someone was there with her. And they could tell her that Miss Na's last word was "Mom."

They phoned us. Did we know such and such a family living under the sacred trees in the Klong Toey slum? We found her mom and relatives under the trees, cooking plain rice, eating it with salt. Nothing else. Scavenging hadn't been good lately.

During those three years, her mom had never visited Miss Na. Not even once. Mom didn't know the bus routes and didn't have enough money for bus fare even if she did. Besides that, Mom's documents were not quite in order. While she was second-generation Thai-born, she never got her documentation in order as the dirt poor don't have money for such things.

Anyway, this team of really caring social workers came from the hospital, and we led them to Mom and told Mom her daughter was dead. They gave her the death certificate, and of course, it being monsoon season, the death certificate got wet in the rain. Plus, Na's brother, high on glue fumes, tore off the dry part of the document and used it for cigarette paper.

That afternoon, after the rain, Mom went with one of our social workers to the hospital, but she could not retrieve the body as she didn't have a death certificate. No documents equals no releasing of the body. Rules, you know. We tried with a copy, but that wouldn't wash. We needed the original.

But no matter, we had prayers at the temple and we made the donation to the monks. It's horrible to be so poor that you don't have enough money for a religious funeral, so we helped, as did some neighbors in the slum.

We couldn't provide all the chants and prayers. You see, for a full religious service you need a body, and we couldn't get the body out of the hospital. So we prayed different prayers quickly in front of the crematorium.

The monks at the local slum-friendly temple were kind. They always are. Again we prayed, as much as is allowed by custom without a body present. Lots of neighbors came. Everyone had heard the story.

The next day we went to the hospital, although her mom didn't dare go because, as I said, Mom herself doesn't have any papers and thus does not exist. They cremated the body of twenty-three-year-old Miss Na. Because it was a no-name body, they put her in a new furnace that wasn't yet tickety-boo, and for which they still needed a couple of bodies to experiment with so they could get the temperature right.

Back with her mom, I recognized Miss Na's picture. She had finished kindergarten at one of our slum schools. Although her mom didn't have a Thai ID card for her, she did have a picture and an ID card written in English from the "Store Front Church" down the street. Her mom just sat there, rocking back and forth, saying over and over, like a chant, "Na, Momma loves you. Momma loves you."

Her real name was Bua, like the lotus flower—beautiful, pure and reaching for the warm rays of the sun. Her little sister is now beginning kindergarten at ten years of age, and maybe there is a chance she can get proper documentation. Her dad once had papers somewhere, in one of the remote provinces. There must be a record somewhere.

# Auntie Jan's New Cell Phone

They knocked down the door, then searched her house and put handcuffs on her second son. Now Auntie Jan will have two of three in prison. Plus six brothers and sisters. More common in our fair land than you would want to think.

Auntie Jan kicked that junkyard dog, who then began severely distracting the arresting officers. That's when she grabbed her son's cell phone. "Mom! Help!" He had whispered to her. Begged her to trash the phone because all his friends' and clients' numbers were in it. It could be used in evidence. Auntie Jan, no stranger to a slum card game and sleight of hand, quickly stashed the phone under the blanket of her AIDS-sick, useless brother-in-law. Shouted at the officers he was highly contagious. She prayed the phone didn't ring.

It wasn't the AIDS that made Auntie Jan's brother-in-law useless. There was more to it. He was out of prison for the third time—drugs, just like all the rest—and was on his way back in. The court didn't know how sick he was when he was sentenced. When the cops found out, they decided they didn't want him to die in jail because there'd be a lot of paperwork. So they turned their backs and he walked away, and they put it in his file that he'd escaped. He had gone to Auntie Jan's for refuge because he was married to her youngest sister, who also was in jail. Father of their two daughters.

The police left with her son, cuffed and sandwiched on the back of a motorbike between two officers, and Auntie Jan retrieved the phone. Trash it? No way. The handcuffs ended any support she'd ever get from that son. You never throw anything away in the slums that might be of some use. If things got really bad, she could sell it to the authorities.

Not that she would. But you never know. In Klong Toey's game of rock-paper-scissors, hunger beats honor and loyalty. Especially if the hungry ones are children, and she was currently caring for four.

Besides, some years from now, once her son gets out, he won't be worth much anyway. Certainly won't find a decent job. To be a tough guy inside, he'll have to get himself an ugly set of tattoos, and once he is released, the tattoos will mark him for life.

First things first. Auntie Jan used the phone to call her niece, Ploy, who was working in Phuket, and told her to come home. Miss Ploy's mother was doing life because she was stupid enough to take that drug rap for Khun Samran, her useless, AIDS-sick, should-be-back-in-jail husband, Ploy's father.

Now Ploy's father, Samran, was dying. AIDS plus TB plus half a pack a day plus an occasional shot of heroin made all that happen. But he was going slow, painfully. He had mumbled that he wanted to see his daughters. Auntie Jan figured that was the proper thing to do: let Miss Ploy and her younger sister Mam take care of their father.

On the all-night bus coming back to Bangkok, Miss Ploy had time to remember what she'd run away from. She'd been about seven when she'd lived with us at the Mercy Centre the first time, but that time too her dad had convinced her to come home to take care of him, cook for him, clean up his mess, quit school, be a servant, run drugs for him.

She did that for five years before he was caught and sent to prison. After that, with her mom already inside, her aunts and uncles wanted her to run their drugs. Have her run their drugs rather than their own kids. Yes, kind of keep things in the family, but one step removed. Better your sister's kids caught than your own. Besides, who cares if a "throwaway kid" with parents in the slammer gets caught? One less mouth to feed. No loss.

That's when Auntie Jan stepped in. Enough is enough. She asked us to take Miss Ploy back. We told her no. Our shelters for kids are operated as open houses, and we didn't have staff to guarantee her safety from the local mafia, who surely wanted her dead. So she was taken into juvenile custody, where she remained for a year.

Upon her release Auntie Jan again asked us to take Miss Ploy, who was now sixteen. We said yes this time because she was no longer "hot material." The drug routes had changed, as they do constantly, and the drug runners no longer considered her a threat because of what she knew. A year later, by the time she was seventeen, and still in one of our shelters, she was in the fifth grade.

But then again, just recently, her daddy's will had prevailed, and again Miss Ploy had returned home, for just a few more runs, he said, until he got on his feet again. She promised to go to school every day. He promised to send her every day and give her lunch money and bus fare. But she began to miss classes, miss being a normal teenager.

When the drug police started sniffing around, Miss Ploy decided she'd had enough. Called us from the Southern Bus Terminal, in tears. Sobbing. Totally without hope. She was on her way to Phuket to work in what she was told was a "traditional" massage parlor, although she had no experience or training. She was told she would never have to "off" (do other things with customers).

That was several months ago. Now, again, a call from home, this time from Auntie Jan. Her father was dying.

In nine years the only time she had seen her mother was for about an hour on some sort of official "family day." She had barely recognized her mom, who was then thirty-two years old. She was totally embarrassed how her mom was carrying on: crying and wanting to hug her, hold her hand—this almost strange woman who said she loved Miss Ploy and younger sister Mam so much.

Old Samran, he always blamed his daughters for his bad luck. It seemed to be the thing he did best; he had a real flair for blaming other people. Oh yes, he was also good at booze and drugs. Besides that, he was a mediocre carpenter. Learned the trade as a kid with his dad but never did much with it until he picked it up again in the prison shop, making furniture, as so many prisoners do.

Miss Ploy remembered all this on the bus, wondering if it could get any worse. Of course it could. It can always get worse in Klong Toey. She hadn't told her Auntie Jan she was pregnant. Three months gone, morning sickness. Fur would fly, and it wouldn't be pleasant.

Her father of course was sicker. Death sick. He was TB coughing and looking awful from the AIDS. On top of that a neighbor had sent his wife over, complaining. She said her husband was training some excellent young fighting cocks for a rich guy, and he figured old sick Samran had the chicken flu or something, and if the birds got the flu or the police came around, they might want him to kill the chickens. Imagine, anyone wanting to put down healthy fighting cocks worth about twenty thousand baht per bird!

Auntie Jan said it wasn't bird flu, it was AIDS and TB. The woman said her husband wanted Samran moved out. He'd even pay Auntie Jan a bit of cash, when the birds got older and when they won some fights and when he got his commission. Hey, a promise of money was better than what she had going for her at the time.

So with Miss Ploy's help they cleaned off an old table and turned it into a bed for him, not too far away and under the old sacred trees. A long time ago there had been a temple there. They had moved the temple, but the trees had remained, growing tall and full and beautiful. Auntie Jan figured that maybe some of the holiness of the trees just might fall down on her useless brother-in-law. Maybe do him some good. They fed him, watered him, looked after him now and then. He was sheltered from the sun and the rain, and it wasn't too hot in the shade. And he had the old junkyard dog for company.

He died, and Auntie Jan and Miss Ploy examined what he'd left behind. A bit of cash, a carton of high-visibility cigarettes, a couple of vials of heroin powder and some antiviral pills. Auntie Jan sold the cigarettes and heroin to a local broker who felt sorry for her. Then she flogged the antiviral pills to a neighbor lady who had the virus. She'd eat a couple of pills each time she met with a customer. Thought they'd keep her from getting AIDS.

The benevolent society provided a casket, and the junkyard dog jumped into the van with the body. Couldn't get him out, so off to the temple. When the temple bells tolled to signal that the cremation was about to begin, he howled like he'd never stop.

Life goes on. With Miss Ploy, Auntie Jan has opened a three-table restaurant by the side of the road, there in the slum. They get along fine and the food is good.

## Auntie Jan's New Cell Phone

Miss Ploy's morning sickness is gone and she studies at home. The wife of the neighbor with the fighting cocks has an education, so she helps Miss Ploy with her schoolwork. She's determined to finish sixth grade. And she says she and the baby in her tummy are cool.

# Crossed off the Night Riders' List

And they came on a no-license motorcycle—the Night Riders—two men on one bike, helmet visors down, the man on the back with a pistol in hand, special 9 mm bullets, ready to shoot. Ready to scratch another name off their "list." It's blood and death when the Night Riders find their man. There's never any mercy. It's a job, a name, that's all. Just meeting their quota for the Biggie Bigs. And so they shot "Motorbike Kheng." Three shots in the head at close range. He was a good man, somebody you'd cheer for if you knew him, somebody who will be greatly missed by family and friends in the "Slaughterhouse" slum here in Klong Toey.

Motorbike Kheng never used drugs in his thirty-one years on earth. He despised drugs. But suspected drug dealers repaired their bikes at his shop. Plus a few motorbike racers and lots of ordinary folks. They shot him anyway. Just for good measure. Just to be sure.

At the time of the killing he was fine-tuning a carburetor on a souped-up 125 cc bike. Squatting, chewing on a toffee, a cell phone to his ear, he had just finished talking with his wife and was saying goodnight to their nine-year-old son. Every evening at nine o'clock, Motorbike Kheng called from his repair shop to say goodnight and three Hail Marys together with his family. His son had just said, "Daddy, I love you," and Kheng had replied, "Daddy loves you too." Those were his last words. Shots rang out. His son screamed, "Mommy, what are those noises in Daddy's shop? They hurt my ears! Why doesn't Daddy talk to me?"

The Night Riders work for someone who seems beyond the reach of the authorities. By day, these cats are smug. Not smirking, but hinting. Not threatening outright, which somehow makes the threats more ominous. They come and talk to the slum community leaders like they would to recalcitrant children, telling our poor neighbors things they already know: that there are still folks flogging drugs in our fair city and all over Thailand. That there are motorcycle shops that "soup up" bikes. All the while ignoring the fact that we all played street football together, grew up together, listened to the same pop songs on the radio. Like they've forgotten where they're from.

Motorbike Kheng was probably a witness to a crime or two. Certainly knew a lot of folks. That's all. Perhaps he knew some things; most likely he didn't. He wasn't that kind of person. Even as a kid, he didn't care about who was dealing, who rode such and such a chopper. It wasn't in his nature. But witness or not, he was on somebody's list, somebody who decided that he wasn't on the right side, and so the Night Riders came.

Motorbike Kheng grew up in the Slaughterhouse. Even as a kid, he could fix anything. He began by fixing bicycles and then progressed to making his own go-karts. He could make a broken Walkman sing. He simply had the knack.

With no dad and a sick mom, he grew up in the care of his aunties. He was always a good kid, polite, didn't cause any problems, didn't hang out with any Slaughterhouse gangs. He hated drugs, never even smoked cigarettes. Only drank a little booze and then only on occasion. He liked to wear his hair long but wore it neat.

His grandmom and three maiden aunties raised him well. He finished the compulsory sixth grade, and then he took a crack at high school and got top scores, but the teachers complained he always came to class with motorcycle grease and grimy fingernails. When he finished his first year of high school, he told his oldest auntie he wanted to work full-time at a neighborhood motorcycle shop. He would finish high school later, he said. One of the aunties felt sad that he wanted to quit school. She never married, never had any children of her own, and she hoped Kheng would be the first man in the family to leave the Slaughterhouse slum to work in an office, maybe as an engineer or a doctor. But she bought him his first set of tools anyway. She shopped carefully and paid ten thousand baht for them. He paid her back in two years, as he had promised.

As the years passed in the Slaughterhouse—with increasing lawlessness, payoffs and all the rest—many of Kheng's friends went down, either to jail or on to the next life. His aunties grew afraid. They urged Kheng to move to a house they had inherited some forty-five minutes away on bus route No. 136. Far away from the Slaughterhouse, to safety, they thought.

After all, motorcycles needed fixing everywhere. Kheng agreed. He was Catholic, and his new home was in a Catholic area, so he got the Catholic bike trade along with those who just came by. It was a modest trade. Just small-time. Living in his aunties' inherited house, tinkering with bikes in the driveway, he made enough to eat and buy a few more tools.

Kheng married a lovely, caring lady, as pretty as pretty gets. She had a son from a previous marriage, whom Kheng gladly took on as his own. Kheng worked in his shop, quietly, for seven years. His reputation grew and made his wife, grandmom and aunties proud. Even the parish priest, who rode a small motorbike around the neighborhood, came and blessed the house and the bike parts scattered around the driveway. Kheng hadn't had a proper church wedding. His aunties said they would speak to the priest; perhaps he could formalize their marriage.

Kheng's old Slaughterhouse cronies continued to get their bikes repaired in his shop, and so did some racing clubs. Kheng never joined a "club" himself, never modified his own bikes to race. But because his bikes would win so frequently, he had instant rich friends and poverty-stricken enemies.

Then there was the issue of his car. A family man, not a hard partying type, he saved some money and used it, together with his wife's small inheritance, to buy a car. Not a new car, just a car. His critics accused him of being "unusually rich." How could a Slaughterhouse kid working in a one-man motorbike repair shop make enough money to buy a car? Had to be drugs, gambling or racing, right? Already more than twenty-five hundred people had been killed in the drug war, and Kheng's name was now added to a list of troublemakers to be dealt with.

And so it began: the harassment. The Night Riders listened to his enemies, saw him as one to be plucked. Started to make visits, borrowed tools. Demanded largesse until it grew out of control. His wife, getting worried, urged him to move: "You grew up in the Slaughterhouse. Let's go home."

She stayed in the aunties' house while Kheng opened up a new shop near the Slaughterhouse, along the old railway line street: five thousand baht per month, including gas and electricity. And his reputation for motorcycle magic followed him. He kept busy.

There is a Thai word: *oom*. It's an ordinary word, meaning to lift up an object, but on the street it means to kidnap a person. Take them away, never to be heard from again.

That's what almost happened about eight months after Kheng opened his new shop. (Or maybe it was a trial run. They often do that.) The Night Riders came, grabbed him, threw him into the back of a pickup, stuck a gun in his ribs, pulled a sack over his head. "Make a noise and you're dead." They demanded thirty thousand baht and he bargained his life with his five-baht gold chain. He'd saved for and bought that chain to give his wife on her birthday. Three weeks later, the Night Riders returned to his shop around nine o'clock, just as he was saying goodnight to his son. They pulled their bike to a stop in front of him, paying no attention to the other customers who were standing around and chatting.

No bargaining this time. They shot him. Three 9 mm bullets behind the ear. And then they leisurely rode away.

Friends rushed Kheng to a private hospital nearby. He was unconscious, possibly brain-dead but still breathing, with blood flowing profusely from his ear. Friends phoned the aunties. There was no doctor in attendance, and the staff said the brain scan machine was broken. Thirty minutes later, after the aunties pooled the gold they were wearing, the machine mysteriously began to work.

They tied Kheng's wrists and feet to the bed as he was writhing about. Outside, eight or so policemen, some in uniform, some not, were milling about. Waiting. Someone remarked that such a display of power for "an accident" with an ordinary citizen seemed a bit unusual.

The aunties were told that the bullets had passed through, did not show on the scan, and that he would probably die with or without an operation, and even if he lived, he would never be the same. The aunties signed for the operation. Feeling that anything is better than death, that with life

41

there is always hope. His friends said they would pay for it on the spot. They pooled their gold. Over ninety minutes had passed when Kheng was finally wheeled into surgery. He died on the operating table.

The aunties and friends followed as the body was moved to a government hospital for an autopsy. There they were told that two bullets were still lodged in Kheng's head, that there never should have been an operation. His situation had been hopeless.

The morning after, the private hospital called the aunties and said there had been an accounting mistake, that they still owed the hospital fifty thousand baht. The aunties returned with a pro bono lawyer. It seemed to be another case of "plucking."

It's been several weeks since the funeral. Kheng's wife, whose loss is truly unimaginable, says that she dreams of her husband every night but that they aren't frightening dreams. In her dreams Kheng smiles and is at peace.

The aunties have taken her in as total family, so she is not alone. The car has been sold. She still lives in the aunties' house along bus route No. 136. She walks with her son to school each morning and then stops at the small Catholic cemetery to lay flowers on his grave. Her son still says his three Hail Marys every night. He says that sometimes, if he prays very quietly to himself, he thinks he can hear his daddy praying with him. But he says it sounds like his voice is far away, muffled, like over the phone.

# Holding on to Pride and Hope

She still hangs on to that old photograph, faded and wrinkled after twenty-five years, of the cab of a long-haul truck. Dad's at the wheel and Mom's snuggled beside him holding their baby, Pou Priew. Now twenty-seven and with a ten-year-old son of her own, Ms. Pou Priew phones her father often. Says he's a gruff dad.

Before the troubles all those years ago, her mother went with her father everywhere, riding shotgun. Mom said that her talking kept him from dozing off at the wheel. He didn't need *ya ba* to stay awake.

Recently Pou Priew rode with her father again on a long-haul run. It was the first time for her son, Prab-pram. It was also the first time the boy had met his grandfather. Prab-pram boasts that he didn't get motion sickness, and it was the first time he had been out of the Slaughterhouse for more than a few hours.

Pou Priew took him along because she was afraid she would go to prison, again, and her son—her only hope—would be abandoned, as she had been when her mother had gone to prison. She wanted him to know his grandpa, who would surely take care of him and send him to the best school he could. He's in the fourth grade now, an honor student.

Riding up front with his mother and grandfather, Prab-pram kept asking for that story again. "The one, Grandpa, about how you and Grandma were so happy together and Grandma was the only woman you ever loved. But how could you love her when she went to prison so often?"

The grandparents had split the sheets twenty-five years before, when Pou Priew was two. That's when her mom began spending most of her time in prison, for drugs.

Today Pou Priew is notorious in Klong Toey for her own jailhouse history—she's had eight spells in prison over eleven years. During her fifth stint, her father came to visit, the only visitor she ever had behind bars. He told her he would send her a little money when he could.

In the cab of the truck Pou Priew whispered to her son that he is her pride and her hope, and it won't always be gambling and drugs and prisons for her.

She is missing a front tooth from a scuffle with a prisoner from another country who outweighed her by fifty kilograms. This woman told her that she was not a good Catholic girl (which she says she is). The ultimate insult. Pou Priew says she won the fight—by smearing smelly mud in her antagonist's eyes.

Twenty-seven years old, she speaks a saucy combo of Slaughterhouse jargon mixed with prison slang. She only finished the third grade. That's when her mother began her "long-term government service" for possession with intent to sell and left nine-year-old Pou Priew pretty much on the street.

The girl later moved in with her grandmother—Shaky Hands Granny, they called her. Granny never missed Sunday Holy Mass, except when she was in the middle of an all-day card game. Granny tried to protect Pou Priew—but one pre-dawn, after the men had finished butchering pigs at the slaughterhouse, when the abattoir was quiet and Granny was next door playing cards, she didn't hear the horrible screams of her granddaughter over the laughter of those four drunks.

Nine-year-old Pou Priew never told Granny. She stole some of Granny's card winnings and got an older girl who worked nights downtown to buy her some medicine.

Years later, as a teenager, Ms. Pou Priew fell in love with a narcotics policeman. Her first real guy—and she really loved him. She named their son Prab-pram which means to "suppress, repress or quash," and, more pointedly, the crime suppression department of the royal Thai police in which his father worked.

When it was time to go to the hospital, her man was gone on police work. Knowing that the baby was coming soon and that he might be away on an assignment, her man had left some money. But she'd spent it all, figuring that since she was nine months pregnant, that should bring some good luck. So she bought a fistful of underground lottery tickets and hit the right numbers. She won a bundle, but the tricky purchase lady wouldn't pay. In desperation, she hocked her husband's two favorite fighting cocks for taxi fare to the hospital, and more.

She gave birth to her firstborn alone—no relatives, no neighbors. She didn't tell anyone she was going to the hospital, and no one was looking in after her. She was so proud of her infant son, said he was going to be a great man. "People will look at me and say, 'There goes Prab-pram's mother.'"

Three nights later, sometime after midnight, she painfully walked out of the hospital, carrying her baby. Why pay if you don't have to? The hospital staff get their salaries no matter what, and they talked trash to her—so she said.

She flagged a taxi to the Slaughterhouse. She still had some cash, but she offered the driver three pills, and, luckily, he agreed. He was a Klong Toey man. He understood. He would have taken her home for free, but why turn down a good deal? Three pills for a fifty baht taxi ride—tourists will pay two to three hundred baht a pill.

Her policeman husband was not pleased with his son's name. Plus he had to go and arrest the guy who had his fighting cocks—for gambling! Of course, he kept the two birds for evidence.

The policeman ditched Pou Priew when Prab-pram was about eighteen months old. They'd been living together as a real family, more or less. He loved her, and he was almost too kind and caring to be a narcotics cop. So why did he leave her? She wouldn't stop gambling, and she was never home. With drugs all around and him charged with investigating them, something had to give.

She moved back into her granny's place with her baby. Pou Priew was always short on cash, and once someone quietly slipped her money to deliver a small newspaper-wrapped package, no questions asked. Her granny was in one of her all-day card games, and Pou Priew stopped by and started betting on Granny—and forgot all about the package. The street kid they'd paid twenty baht to shout if any cops came around had fallen asleep, and the card game was busted.

In the confusion Pou Priew managed to remember the package and stuffed it in Prab-pram's smelly nappy. The police didn't check there, and they let everyone go. However, first they told everyone to empty their pockets and they took all the money. "Take your choice—money or jail," they said.

But now the drugs had poop on them. The seller wanted his drugs back or the money—and she gave him the soiled drugs. He was not pleased.

Not long after that Pou Priew made her first trip to prison. It started with gambling. Granny was a notorious cheat with a deck of cards. No one could catch her. Pou Priew, for all her schemes and scams, is honest. She wouldn't cheat—that was the problem.

She started playing cards and she kept playing, and she kept losing. Finally, to get the cash to play cards, she began to seriously move drugs, then "graduated" to buying and selling. Granny warned her, but she wouldn't listen. She figured her luck would change, and she'd be as good as Granny.

She wasn't happy. Besides losing at cards, she'd also moved in with this new guy who wasn't nice to her. He resented the fact that she was caring for Baby Prab-pram.

Then her luck got even worse and she was busted for drugs, her first conviction. Now the police knew about her. So when she was back on the streets, it was simply a matter of time before they got around to picking her up and charging her again.

One time some "uptown uniforms" gave her some *ber bank* (marked banknotes) to act as their agent and buy from a guy who had started hanging around the five-storey walk-up flats. They said that, if she cooperated with them, they would make all her problems go away. But when she spotted the "mark," she couldn't do it because he had gone to school with Prab-pram's daddy, and his boy and Prab-pram were best buddies in school.

That night her new "live-in" beat her up. He wanted some drugs. So she threw half the marked bills at him and told him to go buy his own. She also let it out that another dealer had set up shop and was cheaper than the mark. Her live-in walked out of the house with the marked bills, and she called the uptown uniforms. Two problems solved.

But the police wanted the rest of the marked bills back, and Master Prab-pram wanted a bicycle for his birthday. She could never say no to her pride and hope.

She went to her granny, now in her eighties, and begged her to get her into one last card game so she could pay the cops their money back, plus have some "coffee money." Granny did it, and she won of course.

The story goes on. Today Pou Priew's life is relatively calm. Prab-pram is still with her in the Slaughterhouse. She's promised to take him on the train down south to stay with her dad awhile. We bought tickets and she pawned them, but she promises they will go soon.

Prab-pram is a son any mother would be proud of. He likes his grandfather and his eighteen-wheel rig. He writes to his grandmother, whom he has never seen, in prison. Granny is healthy and will be released in a few months. She writes back to him every month, and she's excited about seeing him when she gets out.

Grandpa says he still loves Granny, and she can come stay in the South with him. She's a good cook, and so is Pou Priew. They talk about leaving Klong Toey behind and making a fresh start down there, maybe opening up a small food shop in Grandpa's little house facing the big road.

Grandpa knows the headmaster of a good school there, and there's a place in it for Prab-pram if he wants it. The boy says maybe he'll come for a visit on his summer holiday and take another ride in that long-haul truck with Grandpa.

# Last Act of an Almost Magical Finding Stick

She broke it, her almost-magical finding stick. It happened in a panic, while she was frantically prying her rented pushcart off the Klong Toey railway tracks. You can only expect so much from an old piece of bamboo.

The 3:30 p.m. Klong Toey freight train demolished Auntie Chalor's cart. She herself fell backwards to safety when her stick broke. Total disaster—the rented cart was destroyed, her day's rummaging of maybe twenty baht's worth of recyclables ruined. Plus she bruised her bottom when she landed, losing face.

Auntie Chalor has had to support herself ever since her parents died when she was ten and has been a used goods collector and seller for forty-one years. She says that the almost-magical finding stick used all its magic powers at the moment it broke, throwing her back to safety away from the tracks. And that the stick secretly had never gotten along very well with that rented cart anyway. High-class stick, low-class cart.

Even before the train accident her pushcart had a wobbly front wheel and was always breaking down at the worst of times. And with any extra weight on it—like beer bottles, cans, folded-down cardboard boxes or newspapers—she could barely push it. How can anyone make a decent living as a bag lady with a lame cart?

She'd rented her rickety cart from the junkyard guy on Sukhumvit Soi 36 for ten baht a day, and she owed him back rent. She told him that his prices were shameful. Who could possibly pay?

"Prices ain't even prices anymore," lamented Auntie Chalor, a proud descendent of Klong Toey's original Bag Lady Clan. Used newspaper down from five baht a kilogram to one and a half baht, and used-but-washed-clean plastic bags and a case of beer bottles down from fourteen baht to six. And assorted bottles, three for one baht. Cans down too. Plus the junk dealer guy uses a crooked scale to weigh her stuff. Always cheats.

The finding stick was of sturdy bamboo, just the right thickness for her tough, no-nonsense hand grip. Short fingernails. And just the right stubby height, as she is short, maybe 135 centimeters standing straight. She says her mother used to tell her, "You don't have to be tall to be pretty." Mother also taught her how to use a finding stick, with her tagging along behind as her mother stirred through plastic and other recyclables found in rubbish bins and wherever people dump their stuff.

Only glue sniffers stick their bare hands into unknown junk. There are always rats, broken bottles, cans, even snakes—thus, the need for a finding stick. Also, glue sniffers often eat thrown-away food they find. Not Auntie Chalor. Missing a meal or two beats losing dignity.

Once she dug into some rubbish with her finding stick and a young python wrapped itself around it. She shook the stick and hollered at the snake to let go.

After the python incident, she went to the local temple. She carried her finding stick with her so it would touch the sacred ground of the temple. Of course she didn't dare ask for a blessing for the stick, but she felt things got better after the visit.

She had a seizure some years back when she was heavy into the booze and her daughter was small. Ever since then her right side has been weak, and she drags her leg a bit. That was when her husband left her for a younger bag lady—a real hussy!

It wasn't pleasant the first time they met. There were loud words. But what stung the most was her husband was watching, and when the hussy said some bad words ... her husband said nothing. Didn't stick up for her, his major wife. That stung a lot, enough for a lifetime.

She never was married to the man in what society calls a "proper ceremony." Such events cost money and are for "uptown high-society people." Her sister had asked for a 120 baht dowry and there was a bit of quiet talk. The "elders" agreed that the bride's price should be just 80 baht, as Miss Chalor, pretty and young as she was, was "in the family way" and thus slightly used goods. For a wedding ring the bride wore a brass ring she had found with her finding stick, the same ring she still wears today.

Her husband told her before he left her that he didn't want a wife with a gimpy leg. "Gimp or no gimp," she replied, "I'm from one of the oldest families in Klong Toey, and you'd better appreciate that." But he didn't. Her sister always said that the man was low in station.

But life goes on, and while the junk dealer didn't charge her then and there for the destroyed cart, he did tell her he'd have to raise her daily rent to fifteen baht a day until the cart was paid for. She cursed him, calling for every demon who lives in garbage bins to come out to haunt him. Even after the train crash and Auntie Chalor's trash talk, he did let her rent another cart, but only one in slightly worse condition. He told her that at an extra five baht a day it would take 120 days' rent to pay for another cart. She doesn't talk to him now, gives him "the silent treatment."

Her daughter helped her take the smashed cart back to the junk dealer. Tied it to the back of a motorcycle. She is eighteen, pretty, and everyone calls her a "tom." Wears her jeans slung low on the hip, boy-style, and spikes her hair. Says Klong Toey boys are sissies who are trying to act tough. They smoke expensive three baht cigarettes out of a pack and have tattoos—fake ones, not one of the big nine tattoos that can really protect you.

At eighteen she feels embarrassed to help her mom push the cart, says her school friends laugh at her. And her mom tells her: "Shush, shush. Such talk! We are an old family of Klong Toey with a dignified profession. People know us. We have a reputation to uphold."

The train accident happened the afternoon before the last full moon. On the following evening Auntie Chalor placed a bucket of water out in the moonlight. Early dawn, before the moon went away, she bathed in the water shone on by the moonlight, hoping that she would be protected from further cart accidents.

Auntie Chalor never went to school. She wanted to, but the school said she needed a Thai birth certificate. She had one, but when she was one year old, her parents' shack burned down in a Klong Toey slum fire; their clothes and documents went up in smoke. So her parents chalked it up to bad karma and decided their daughter wouldn't need a birth certificate. Later her dad died "of an age" and her mother got drunk one afternoon, fell in the Prakanong canal and didn't come up. Auntie Chalor was ten.

She can't read, but she knows her "sums"—oh boy, does she ever know her sums! She has to with that cheating junk dealer guy and his crooked scales.

There are a couple of things Auntie Chalor talks about. When you ask about the dangers of her profession, the first thing she says is she hasn't been bitten by a dog in years. She credits that to the fact that she's never even once eaten dog meat. That's what they say in Klong Toey—eat dog meat even once and the dogs know forever and will bite you.

And then there's the husband who dumped her for that hussy—she talks about him too. She says she knows now why they split. It was because their celestial signs clashed. She should have known better, should have checked him out. But she was young then, and that's a story for another day. These days she's more careful, more worldly, and now she wears *sai sin*, the wristband of string you get from the temple when you make merit. Says it protects her and makes her feel more confident.

Last time she passed by our Mercy Centre, she told me the tale about her flip-flops and the glue sniffer. The day before, just halfway through her daily six-hour sojourn for recyclable secondhand goods, one of her flip-flops came loose. The right one. That's her bad leg side, the side that takes the most punishment. The thong between her first and second toes came out. And new rubber flip-flops are horribly expensive. Thirty-nine baht, maybe more.

She was sitting along the roadside, trying to do a repair job with some string, tie it together somehow, when this glue sniffer ambled by—watched her a while. He wasn't totally hammered yet, else he would have been skittish and into his own world. He knew Auntie Chalor. She'd helped him a while back when he'd really needed some glue to get through the day. She'd found an old can with some glue still in it, saved it for him when he needed it. He was grateful. He remembered.

Now, glue sniffers don't pour the whole can into their plastic sniffing bags—maybe about a third, and they cap the rest till they need more. So this glue sniffer, remembering, opened his can and found a twig along the road, and then he and Auntie Chalor fixed the thong—glued it back together. He waited with her till the glue dried and she could wear her rubber flip-flops again for a while.

With prices for secondhand goods having plummeted, she's back more and more on the street. Stashes her cart and tote on the footing of an expressway pillar along the slum canal. Doesn't eat at her sister's shack anymore—comes back late when her sister and daughter are asleep and leaves again before dawn, so as not to bother anyone. Embarrassed, but with a grin, she says it's only a matter of time till prices go up and she gets back on her feet again.

# PART II

The Heroes and the Almost Heroic
Among Us

# The Left-Handed Artist of Klong Toey*

**V**iolence and mayhem don't "just happen" in our slums. They're not how we handle our affairs. When they do occur, they can almost always be attributed to outside causes. This was the case for Klong Toey's Khun Dhee, whose life descended into mayhem during the Red Shirt demonstrations two years ago.

Dhee was hit by shrapnel from an old tear-gas canister during a fracas. The effects of these weapons are insidious— you can't breathe, smoke sears your lungs and your eyes, and the chemicals mixed in with the shrapnel burn deep to scar, maim and cause wounds that won't heal.

An artist and portrait painter, Dhee bore the entire vicious brunt of the tear-gas grenade. Shrapnel tore his right lung, bruised and cracked some ribs, breaking one, and mangled his right hand. A couple of pieces penetrated his chest and throat, bringing him to his knees.

He kept his head back to make it easier to breathe and clasped his good hand to his throat, trying to ease the pain. He never lost consciousness during those first few minutes and kept a tight grip on his motorcycle key with a sacred image attached.

---

*This is the story of the artist Mr. Chingchai Udomcharoenkit, whose illustrations are featured in this book.

Later, eyes swollen from the searing tear gas, all he could think of was his wife, Mam, and his sons, Blue and Jazz, waiting for him at home. He didn't know how badly he was wounded and thought he could still manage to ride his motorbike.

Dhee married Mam thirteen years ago, and before marriage they had a nine-year courtship. In those thirteen years of marriage, they had not been apart for a single night. When he didn't come home and didn't phone, Mam feared the worst.

Our old friend Mr. Mah, head of the Klong Toey Emergency Relief team ambulance service, was just a stone's throw away from where Dhee was hit. He heard the gunfire, saw the exploding canisters and was blinded a bit by the gas.

As Dhee lay wounded, folks gathered around him—Red Shirts, Yellow Shirts, men in uniform, all briefly united, everyone shouting to hurry up, to get Dhee to a hospital. Everyone shouting for Dhee not to die. People from all groups promised to pay his hospital bills, no matter what. Everyone wanted to touch the wounded semiconscious Dhee to give him the strength and courage to survive as they loaded him into the ambulance.

Mah (a nickname meaning "loyal, protective dog") had someone else drive while he cradled Dhee in his arms, holding his head with his hand so that the wounded artist could breathe

"Dhee, you're going to be OK. You're safe," Mah said. "You know me. I used to buy noodles from your dad's shop in Klong Toey. I used to take you to school sometimes."

And Dhee scribbled one word on a bloody piece of paper with his left hand: "Mam."

"Just please try to keep breathing," Mah said. "I'll get you home."

Twenty minutes later they had arrived at the emergency room of the nearest hospital. Mah had phoned ahead, but the hospitals were already on red alert. (They took him to the very hospital he'd been in that same morning visiting the wounded—those wounded on the same streets.)

Thirteen hours in surgery, and Khun Dhee lived. The surgery team later joked in gallows humor how they cried their eyes out as they "repaired" him. But it wasn't from sorrow; he reeked of tear gas.

He was to be in the hospital for two-and-a-half months and eight more operations. He's now back home in the flats in Klong Toey, living with his wife and his sons, Blue and Jazz, still drawing and still painting portraits, perhaps just as well as before, maybe better, but surely slower now with his left hand.

He had always been a right-handed artist. He began relearning to draw a full month after he left intensive care, with armed men waiting outside his door. Then, in a room of his own, still in hospital, he picked up a pencil and began drawing. With his wife patiently sitting beside him, helping him, it took him the next three months, sixteen hours a day, to learn to draw with his left hand.

Slowly the miracle happened. His left-handed drawings were becoming as beautiful as his right-handed ones had been before.

Dhee's been a stubbornly hard worker all his life, even as a little kid. Selling flower garlands on slum street corners. Working as a "bus boy" on the old red clunkity-clunk Klong Toey baht buses. He became a novice monk at nine years old for a month to make merit for his mom when she died. Dropped out of school after that—in the third grade—to help his dad set up their street corner noodle shop, consisting of two tables and six chairs, open nightly from six to ten. His dad, born in mainland China, always smoking and coughing, wasn't that strong anymore.

At nine years old Dhee was a noodle shop helper with his dad by night and a kid coolie in the Klong Toey port by day—a go-for-this, go-for-that errand boy, running up and down gangplanks of the cargo ships. Whatever any of the men or women wanted, he got for them. Quick service. Cash up front of course.

That's when he first started drawing. He'd draw with the stub of any pencil on any scrap of paper he could find. Then one of the men at the port bought him a pad of drawing paper and a couple of pencils, and Dhee was on his way, drawing everything he saw, learning to illustrate, shade, add texture, create art. It changed his life. That's why he was there during Bangkok's troubles—to tell at least some of the story in sketches. That's how he got his right hand blown off.

Back when he was nine, he started sketching portraits of the men at the port working—loading and unloading ships, sitting, eating, talking, playing cards, everything, all the everyday life. They'd give him maybe ten or fifteen baht for the portraits, depending on whether they had any money. And Dhee'd give the money to his dad.

But back to that night of violence and mayhem. I haven't told you yet about how Mam found out about Dhee. It wasn't cool. When he didn't come home, she panicked and started phoning all of his artist friends who might have been with him. Nobody knew anything.

Then came a phone call. Someone's girlfriend had just seen a news flash in England and called long distance to Thailand. Her artist boyfriend was Dhee's friend. She told her boyfriend that she saw Dhee wounded, being loaded into an ambulance. The boyfriend called Mam, and Mam found the hospital.

At first staff at the hospital reception were cautious. Was she his wife? After a battery of questions they finally said, "Yes, fine, but he's still in surgery." She was there when he regained consciousness.

A real shock came with the next morning's Thai newspapers. Dhee was on the front page of one, and pointing to his mangled hand holding a key, the newspaper suggested that his own bomb had gone off before he could toss it. Painting him as a terrorist, the paper suggested his injuries were of no great loss—*good riddance to bad rubbish.*

But he wasn't holding the key to a bomb. It was his motorcycle key with a sacred image.

Mah, who took him to hospital, and the team of surgeons who operated on him, later testified that in his clasped fist were a motorcycle key and a sacred image on a key chain. He also had a mobile phone hanging from a cord around his neck, blown to pieces by the shrapnel, that had most surely protected him from more chest wounds.

The newspaper later apologized. Dhee never took them to court for defamation. He said the Thai equivalent of that old motto: "Least said, soonest mended."

We in Klong Toey rarely kill each other. We govern ourselves as we have since the old days—Klong Toey justice. The first resort is a bottle of local whiskey, ice and soda and hours of street corner horse-trading. What is said in a Klong Toey street corner whiskey and horse-trading session stays there. Not spoken of again. In most matters this kind of problem-solving can be much more effective than that undertaken in police stations and law courts.

Dhee, now forty-five, lives a quiet life but remains busy as an artist in the flats. His boys are now eight and ten. His wife Mam looks after the family, while Dhee works steadily at the drawing table in their flat.

## The Left-Handed Artist of Klong Toey

In many wonderful ways Dhee is the essence of Klong Toey, where beggars are also poets and bag ladies sing songs of life and the music between earth and sky. A place full of mothers and grandmothers, where children are still mostly safe. Klong Toey, a place that anyone around the world who plays music on street corners and draws pictures and paintings on city pavements would like to experience. A place of no polish, no refinement, where the language is colorful and you don't need to wash your ears.

Dhee is there in the flats. Yes, along with a few rats and cockroaches, but they have their place too.

# A Teacher Like Her Mother Before Her

"Teacher! Miss teacher! Miss teacher! You be teacher!" That's what an old crazy woman who lived under the Three Soldiers Bridge used to shout at Lek. As early as she remembers, every time she walked by that bridge, the old lady would turn those words into a chant, "You be teacher! You hear me? You be teacher!" And so she is today, but nowhere near the Slaughterhouse or the Three Soldiers Bridge.

Now she rides a long-tail boat forty-five minutes each school day from the city of Ranong to the island of Koh Lao, where she teaches sixty sea gypsy kids in a rickety wooden shack that floods ankle-deep in the high tides. Sometimes the moms have to carry the kids on their backs, wading thigh-deep in the water, from their stilt shacks to the rickety school.

Khru Lek is a gifted teacher. Brilliant. Even magical. And the sea gypsy children adore her. Her school children can say with pride, "We learn to count, to read, to write our own names, to dance, to sing, to tell stories, to play new games, to brush our teeth, to fight germs, to say nice words, to make friends." When Khru Lek teaches the children how to count, they in turn teach her the numbers in their own Moken sea gypsy language.

Khru Lek is a widow. In the slums they would call her a single mom. True, she had two children by her man—each between his prison terms. However, there was no wedding. No parental blessings. Khru Lek and her "companion" rented a shack, but Lek's mom, Khru Duang, never approved of the arrangement. Neither did her dad.

Lek's dad really disliked this companion. Wouldn't let him set foot in their home. He told Lek: "If this companion of yours sets one foot in our shack, I will shoot him with my .44 and feed him to the hungriest fish in our *klong*." Lek's dad was a gun-carrying narcotics cop.

Eventually Lek's dad did get to shoot him, but not for coming into the house. That never happened. Lek's companion went down in a drug battle. Khru Lek believes he drowned in the *klong*, taking a bullet or two on the way. That's the way she dreamed it that night, after the gun battle. Nobody knows for sure. It all happened so fast, with lots of shooting on both sides, the companion fellow fleeing toward the *klong* with a pocketful of drugs and an illegal .38 he'd taken off a wounded policeman years before.

Lek's companion, the father of her two children, kept shooting at the cops over his shoulder and running as the cops, led by Khru Lek's dad, were closing in, guns blazing, bystanders screaming. He either jumped or stumbled over the bank of the *klong* on the Slaughterhouse side, across from Wat Saphan, in the deepest part of the *klong*, the spot that holds the legend of the hidden alligators.

In fact no one has seen an alligator around there for years. But no body floated to the surface on the night of the gun battle or in the days that followed. Not that anyone looked very hard, but nevertheless, there was no body and no evidence of this guy's death, though there was a trail of blood leading to the bank where he jumped.

# Part II: The Heroes and the Almost Heroic Among Us

On the night her man disappeared, Lek had been standing on the bank, not far from her dad, when a friend beside her urged her to dump her drug stash. A few cops overheard, but she was the daughter of a cop, and her man was the only one to go down. They gave her a little space.

Lek's dad caught drug guys, a job in the slums that comes with several perils and temptations. On the night Lek's companion went down, Lek's dad was already tottering in his job. Sometimes he didn't bring the "product" to the police station to be weighed, counted and photographed. And somehow he always had a pocketful of ready cash offered by some of the better-heeled drug folks he caught red-handed. On the way to the police station, cash made the product disappear.

Then one day Lek's dad got tempted and tried a bit of the product. Then another day and another, and one day he awoke totally addicted. That's how it began for him, much the same way it began for his oldest beloved daughter, Lek, born to be a teacher, as that old crazy lady used to shout at her. Lek slithered down that long drug path for seventeen tortuous years.

Let me tell you about her promise, a promise to quit drugs that took her seventeen years to keep. You could say her addiction was her own fault. We all have our choices.

Lek's dad, as a narcotics cop and a drug user, always had a small stash of product in the house before he turned in state's evidence. Even though he went after bad guys who sold drugs to kids, he told his own daughter she could try a bit of product if she wanted, but to be careful. Lek wasn't careful. Not at all. And after her companion "disappeared" into the *klong*, she began mainlining.

Her mom, Khru Duang, would scream at her and throw the product in the toilet. Then her drug cop dad would go into a rage at Khru Duang, saying, "You're throwing away money! And lots of it!" He'd rage on. How was he supposed to get promoted for catching bad guys if his own wife was going to throw away his promotion, and the evidence? Plus he could sell the product on the side, make enough so she didn't have to work, teaching all those snotty-nosed kindergarten kids always tramping through the house. And with her husband in a rage, all Khru Duang could do to fight back was to go out and buy him strong whiskey so he would drink and pass out.

As Khru Lek's addiction got worse, Khru Duang begged her daughter to promise to stop. Khru Duang is almost Catholic—she has a few Catholic relatives—so she insisted that her daughter make the promise before a statue of the Blessed Virgin Mary. And since Lek and her children are Buddhist, she also made the promise, kneeling together with her two children, before a statue of Buddha.

The only thing that saved daughter Lek was her mother's insistence to keep the promise. Khru Duang never gave up on her daughter. And her daughter never forgot her promise. During all those years Khru Duang always provided food for her drug-addicted daughter, always left a cozy place for her to sleep beside her shack. On the buggiest nights Khru Duang even gave her daughter mosquito nets, but Lek always sold them for drugs. Khru Duang never cursed her daughter and never abandoned hope.

In the end Khru Duang's narcotic-cop husband never got his promotion and was rousted out of the force. Unemployed, drinking hard, he had a stroke about ten years ago and has been paralyzed and helpless ever since. He slurs his speech—you can barely understand what he says now—and maybe that's for the better. We don't know why his wife, Khru Duang, cares for him. She has stood by him, even after he pretty much destroyed everything sacred in their family and added ruin to the police force and their slum neighborhood.

As for Lek, after seventeen years on every kind of drug imaginable, her destiny on this planet was still to be a kindergarten teacher, like her mom before her. About a year ago Ms. Lek began scratching and crawling her way back. She quit drugs by herself, but what got her to quit was what happened to her daughter.

It went down like this. Lek had been hanging out near the sacred shrine outside the new flats across from the pigpens. There's always fresh garbage there, some of it edible. Her old, lame, one-eyed dog was beside her. The dog always protected Lek. Most days, when she and her dog were hungry, they'd do the garbage bins together. On that particular day, she hated herself for feeling so sick and miserable. She was retching in agony, sick from a bad batch of heroin. In between bouts of retching she heard a rumble of voices as a small crowd gathered nearby. One of the noodle stall ladies hollered at Lek, "You better get over there to the pens. It's your daughter."

Lek stumbled over to the holding pens. The daily delivery of just over two thousand pigs had just been trucked in, counted, weighed and prepared for the night's butchering. There, lying on the ground, she saw her brother, drug drunk, stuck halfway into a trough that carries out the leftovers into the canal after the nightly butchering. And there, a few feet away from her brother, was her own fifteen-year-old daughter—dazed, delirious, whimpering. Her clothes in tatters, she had been raped by her uncle.

Lek grabbed a nearby bamboo pole—one of the poles they use to herd the pigs off the trucks and down the wooden ramps to the butchering pens—and began beating him with it. But she couldn't even hold the pole straight, didn't have the strength after seventeen years of drugs. And then she burst into tears because she couldn't beat him to death. She tried to soothe her daughter, tried to hug her, but her daughter screamed, "I hate you, Mom. Get away from me!"

A few kind neighbors took Lek's daughter to the hospital. Cops came by and took Lek's brother to the police station. Lek was left all alone. Even her dog ran away. Hours later, her mom, Khru Duang, came by. She had been to the hospital. Her granddaughter was OK, kind of.

But Lek was a mess. Khru Duang half-carried and half-dragged her daughter, born to be a teacher, back to her shack. Then she tied Lek to a pole outside their shack to keep her from running away or hurting herself during withdrawal. She kept her tied up that way for several days, and kept reminding her of her promise as Lek cursed the day, cursed the night and cursed her promise. The neighbors complained a lot about the noise, the screaming and moaning. Some even threatened to hit her with a pole if she wouldn't shut up. That only made Lek scream louder.

Finally Lek felt better. But she still hated herself for never being a good mom for seventeen years. Instead, her own mom had raised the children, always waiting for Lek to come home and keep her promise. And so far she has kept it. She hasn't touched drugs since she was tied to that pole. Lek's daughter is also OK. She's back in school, living with her granny, Khru Duang.

And Khru Lek, she's down in Ranong, teaching sea gypsy kids. She plans to return to Klong Toey someday, but not too soon. Feels she's not quite strong enough right now. But there will come a day when she will come back, and perhaps she will bring her sea gypsy school children to meet her mom and show them Klong Toey and the Slaughterhouse, where she grew up. It's not easy growing up here. Klong Toey, especially the Slaughterhouse, can be a savage place.

It's like the line from that beautiful Irish song: "A savage place, drenched in decency."

# Don't Be Like Me

We didn't torch the shack after he died. Wanted to. Should have. How else do you get rid of years of tuberculosis? So, next-best, we bagged everything—mattresses, bedding, mosquito nets and clothing. Everything you could put a match to. Brought it out of the shack and burned everything in the street. Didn't want to hurt Sam, an adolescent python.

We told the man's two girls that their teddy bears must go too. A huge crying jag followed. Sure, his two daughters were sixteen and twenty and rumored to be runners, as they say in the drug business. But a teddy bear is a teddy bear, especially when you grow up too fast, and teddy is the only good memory of a not-much-fun childhood.

Mr. Lek (RIP) died at age forty-six, drunk for the last twenty-four years of his life. His wife, Tuk, was once the prettiest girl on this side of the Chao Phraya River. She came to the temple for his cremation.

A day or so after he died, the Health Department appeared. Masks, gloves and disinfectant. But the daughters wouldn't let them spray. They worried that it might hurt Sam, the half-grown python who lived peacefully in his part of the shack, where part of the wooden floor had rotted and sagged. Lived between the floor and the stagnant water under the house.

Sam feasted on rats and other such critters. Protected the shack, really. Let me explain. What with Lek's TB and all the whiskey he drank, after Tuk moved out, the shack was never too clean. But once Sam the python moved in, the house stopped being roach- and rodent-friendly. Sam was also great for the daughters, who came and went as semi-active runners and would often hide a stash in the house. With Sam around, casual visitors were rare.

Still, the girls never really liked Sam and didn't like to sleep there. He scared them. With Dad coughing his lungs out plus his booze cronies, plus a half-grown python, it was not an ideal home for young girls.

In his younger days Lek had shown great promise. As a student, for two years running his scores were among the highest in the Kingdom. He was also an activist, one of the young teenage idealist leaders who spearheaded the slum movement that brought water, electricity, government schooling and proper house registration to Klong Toey, during and after the October Un-Pleasantness some thirty years ago. But none of this counts here in Klong Toey, or anywhere really, when you lose your wife by neglect and your daughters have to survive on the streets.

As a young man, Lek took the civil service application test. He was already drinking, couldn't stop, but scored the highest ever. Some prudish folks at the office shuddered that an outsider could be that smart, so they had him come in second. That barb always stung his pride. He talked about it a lot. That plus his ten months as a freedom fighter against the communists in Laos.

Before the illness and the booze Tuk gave birth to two healthy daughters, Gif and Puey. Then came the TB. Lek didn't take his meds seriously and regularly. Fatal neglect.

He died nine years ago this month. The day after the cremation, Tuk officially remarried and left her children to fend for themselves. Today she's fifty years old, and her daughters, Ms. Gif and Ms. Puey, are twenty-nine and twenty-five. Such things as a quick marriage to a man ten years younger one day after the cremation of a first husband we all understand. On the other hand, abandoning her daughters was harsh. Luckily, both girls had learned long before that they had to make their own way.

Gif, the eldest, inherited her daddy's brains, plus his addiction. Puey, the youngest, also inherited the brains, plus her mom's beauty, but without the addiction. And so it began.


Ms. Gif hardly cracked a book in high school. Still somehow she graduated at the top of her class and was chosen Smartest and Most Popular Girl. But there was no money for school tuition. The game is simple. Students can study and come to school, yes, but if they don't pay the tuition, there is no diploma, no gown and no graduation ceremony. That broke Gif's heart.

At the time, Mom was gone and Dad was drunk. Gif went to a drug thug whom she had been doing errands for occasionally. Asked him to help pay school tuition so she could graduate with honors. He turned her down. Laughed at her, sneered and suggested some intimate favors.

That next week she heard about a shipment. She wrote a snitch note with very clear handwriting, and the drug thug bled to death on the street in a hail of 11 mm bullets, specially modified to kill, waiting for an ambulance that would never come. Stuck in traffic. Ms. Gif was fifteen years old at the time.

In and out of a slum drug commune, she got pregnant. Her son is now twelve. Although at the top of his class, he is not nearly as smart as his mom. Also doesn't show her enough respect. It will take him some time and some tears and some years to realize that, no matter what, she is his mom and she'd die for him, that maybe she can't give up drugs for her son, but at least she'd try.

Three years ago word was going around on the street in Klong Toey about a list of names the drug thugs had produced. The foolish ones felt their tattoos and amulets would protect them, forgetting that those police used 11 mm bullets specially designed to kill despite the protection promised by tattoos and amulets. The message from the police was clear enough. "Have to shoot a few people. Nothing personal." The new police orders came from upstairs—don't bother with other, normal criminal activities; just concentrate on drugs.

But although prices skyrocketed and blood flowed on the streets, drug use and distribution merely changed gears. Quieter and less flamboyant, Ms. Gif began hanging out more at the tourist bars. One night she tripped on "ice" with this tourist guy. Early the next morning she came home to Klong Toey hallucinating. Freaking out, she jumped off a footbridge with a five-meter free fall to the street below, bounced off a car and broke her back. They put a steel rod in her back at the Police Hospital.

The arresting officer was a good and gentle man, originally from Klong Toey. When he saw her last name, he realized he had fought alongside her dad in Laos. He wrote up in the report that she'd been drunk at the time of the incident.

She came to us to recover for four months, till they removed the steel rod. Now, as I write this in November 2007, she is addicted to methadone, which is reasonably easy to obtain. She lives with her old boyfriend, the father of her son. He is now mostly clean, and he's trying to get her to stop. There is always hope.

Another accident happened more recently while she was on a paid errand for a drug thug. Riding sidesaddle on a motorbike, a car sideswiped them. At the hospital, fearing the worst, she told the emergency room staff that she would pay out of her own pocket.

A couple of mornings later, the hospital accountants came to her bedside asking for fifty thousand baht. Gif phoned her sister, Puey, to bring her some clothes. At noon Gif went to the bathroom, dressed in the nice clothes her sister had brought, combed her hair like in her sister's ID picture and walked out. Collected her sister's ID card from the guards.

Hospital staff phoned us. Asked us if we knew her.

"Yes."

Do we know where she is?

"No."

They said they'd have to go to the police to collect the money.

We said, "Good luck."

As for Ms. Puey, Ms. Gif's younger sister, she's now twenty-five and has a beautiful seven-year-old daughter who has all her mom's beauty and brains. Puey is now in her third year in university. She struggles a bit because she fast-forwarded from sixth grade to university with a bit of private tutoring on the side.

Puey met her daughter's father when she was fourteen and gave birth at seventeen. They "split the sheets" long ago while she was still pregnant. Said she would not move drugs while she was pregnant. Didn't seem proper.

Also, the drug thug she had dealt with blinked. Pregnant Puey witnessed the men on the motorcycle armed with the 11 mm bullets specially designed to kill. Saw the blood on the street. She promised the baby in her tummy she would never deal with drugs again. She moved in with her grandma. Pawned her gold and nice clothes. Poor again, she got a job washing dishes at a sidewalk noodle stand for food money. Gave birth to her daughter in the charity ward of a nearby hospital.

We met Puey one day several years ago and asked her if she was clean. She said she'd been clean for years, which was true.

Then opportunity came. There was a scholarship opening. She was the brightest, and we contacted some special tutors to get her, at warp speed, up for university-level academia.

Why do I tell you this story about the two daughters? Their dad was a flawed hero, and Klong Toey is harsh to its fallen idols. He harped at his girls, "Don't be like me." And all he gave them was his shame and a daily dose of failure. It's a true story. And more than that, it's about all of us.

Ms. Gif is trying to quit still one more time. Will she stop? Probably not. They offer her methadone, but methadone is what she's addicted to. But she loves her son and takes care of him the best she can.

Ms. Puey loves her daughter and they are cool together, though they may never ever really get along because they are so much alike.

And Gif and Puey's mom—Mrs. Tuk, the widow who remarried the day after the cremation—well, her new husband isn't the best man on the block, but he does love her and he doesn't drink.

Puey is totally determined to graduate. Gif has promised to be there, to be family. To see her little sister wear the graduation gown that she never wore. Their children will be there too, and they will bring a picture of a young Mr. Lek in his jungle fatigues when he was a freedom fighter against the communists in Laos. The policeman who took Gif to the hospital when she jumped off the footbridge has promised to come with some old hands who fought alongside their dad. Mom won't be invited because, simply, she abandoned them. But her daughters will be terribly disappointed if she doesn't show up.

It's never a true state of despair. It could be, but we can't let that happen, can we?

# The Junk Man and His Most Precious Throwaway Kid

He was an old drunk who had sobered up as much as he could. He still swayed a bit, I think mostly out of habit. He hadn't cried in years, but embarrassed tears rolled down his face out of love for the little girl Kaewalee.

Called her his daughter, you know, for the children he never had. A confirmed bachelor, always said no decent lady would look twice, even once, at the likes of him. Illiterate. Never went to school. No documents. Not handsome—a junk man. So he lived his life alone. In his shack there beside the Klong Toey slums, in the grove of sacred trees next to where Kaewalee and her family stayed. Totally surrounded by used materials—plastic bags by the kilo, tin cans, beer bottles, scrap wire, etc.—that he had not yet got around to selling. Or waiting for the price to go up a baht or so per kilo.

It's known as a sacred place. Although now gone, a temple once stood there. Sacred trees are common to temple compounds. Not unusual to find old Buddhist amulets.

Kaewalee simply thought of him as Uncle and was always polite like her momma told her to be. Her momma used to whomp her alongside the head when she wasn't. That was before Momma went to prison. Momma didn't do drugs, didn't sell drugs, but she'd keep them for the neighbors.

One day the police came. There was screaming, shouting, dogs barking. Everyone said Momma was innocent, and she was, but ... The policeman found drugs in Momma's dirty clothes basket.

Kaewalee never laughed at Uncle, at his clothes and long hair. When he fell drunk outside his shack, she woke him up and got him inside. Even chased off the stray wild dogs when they snarled. She had a way with them. Even the most ferocious would obey her. And the police didn't bother Uncle. They knew he'd lived in that sacred grove for years. Had no documents, but everybody knew him. And as long as he didn't bother anyone ...

He was generous with whatever he had and almost always had five baht in his pocket for the beggars—"the poor," as he called them—whom he met along the way. His own average income was less than twenty baht a day.

Most often, "the poor" wouldn't accept anything from him. They knew him, and there is honor and dignity among the poorest of the poor. They might share a five-baht plastic bag of cooked rice and some fish sauce.

Kaewalee was often sent to the local temple to collect the leftover food from the monks. She would always stop on the way home and share a bit with Uncle.

When she was little and her mom and dad were sleeping off a drinking binge, Uncle would take her and her brother off at first morning light in his junk cart, both half-asleep—early morning foraging, so he'd be there first when the junkyard owner opened up. Uncle soon found a few items not attached to anything. Enough for a few baht to buy them something to eat. Sometimes just rice and fish sauce. But that works well when you're really hungry.

It wasn't long after Momma went to prison that Kaewalee came to live with us. She had nowhere else to go, really. Dad had died and her brother was on the street. She was almost twelve and her dream was to learn to read and write. She'd never been to school, but she knew another girl from the sacred grove who was already going to our special school. Kaewalee lived with us for eight months. Happy and in school. Her dream had come true.

But now she is gone. Cremated in a donated coffin at the Temple by the Bridge—the local temple known to ruffians, hooligans, gangsters, saints and the poor. No longer there to protect Uncle. Strange how she had this gift with animals, especially stray dogs.

So Uncle picked up this throwaway stick plus a sturdy walking one. Now, he knows his sticks because a three-wheel pushcart junk man needs something sturdy to deal with bothersome stray dogs. You would think that stray junkyard dogs would cozy up to stray junkyard men, but they don't.

No need to whittle the stick to a point because it's soft ground there under the sacred trees. They had a fire there a while back. It burned down about a dozen shacks, scorched a couple of trees. We garnered a bit of money and rebuilt the shacks, and now with the monsoon rains coming early, two of the biggest trees are coming back. Bits of green on the branches.

Everyone had said the trees were dead. Except Uncle. He'd put joss sticks and candles in front of the trees, telling them he was sorry and please don't go away. Uncle and the trees and the community had lived together a long time.

He'd bought a ten-baht garland that morning. Hey, that's why he was a bit sober. The garland instead of the booze. He didn't have the courage, the strength, to go out with his junk cart. Afraid of the dogs. Afraid of everything. Without this little girl, Kaewalee, who lived in the sacred grove in a two-hundred-baht lean-to shack.

She was that important to him, even though she wasn't his daughter. He stuck the pointy end in the ground and hooked the garland on top with a rubber band, with an unlit cigarette in the middle. Yes, she'd been just twelve and hadn't smoked. But in matters of the next world, well, you never know.

He's a man of simple religion, and that was his way of properly saying goodbye. Even if he did smoke the cigarette himself. After all, it was an expensive cigarette. One of those from a package—two baht and a half for one cigarette and five baht for two. Also he bought a five-baht plastic bag of cooked rice. Put that on the stick also and then ate it. That is acceptable in the lore under the trees in the sacred grove.

He'd park his pushcart near the hospital and wait for news. And after she died, he and his cart stayed outside the temple. He wouldn't go in because he was afraid they'd shoo him out. With his clothes and haircut he didn't want to be an embarrassment to Miss Kaewalee. That would be terrible. Her family never did like him. Always hollered and cursed her when she gave him some of the temple rice left over from the monks. They told her that's why their dogs barked and snarled at him, because Kaewalee gave the rice to him instead of their two dogs.

As he told us later, there was something he didn't know. After death, lying there in her donated casket, could she still control the stray temple dogs? Protect him from them?

Anyway, he didn't know how to act there in the temple. He said that he didn't know any prayers, never had been ordained a monk as a boy. Family was too poor.

Uncle said his secret wish was to become a monk before the casket to make merit for her. Just even for the three days till the cremation. But he thought his head was too thick, as they say, like a water buffalo, and he couldn't memorize the prayers and thought that he was too old, and even if he asked, the monks might gently refuse him. So in the end he didn't dare.

Also he didn't think it proper to bring his sturdy stick into the temple proper. No weapons, you see. But the strays were strangely silent, even though the three days they waked Miss Kaewalee at the temple were the time of the full moon. A couple even came and slept beside him and his cart. He stayed there just outside the temple for the three nights, keeping vigil.

Everyone called her Kaew. Short for Kaewalee. Her whole life, she had answered to that sound. As far as she knew, her official name was Kaewalee Chareonsuk.

Documents such as birth certificates, house registration and identity cards were not heavy-duty, industrial-sized priorities in her family. Besides, living in a two-hundred-baht claptrap lean-to shack, where do you keep such things? To keep them away from the rain. From the mice and rats and creepy-crawlies that love the taste of document paper.

At Kaewalee's birth her mom could not afford the minimal payment in the welfare section of the maternity ward of the government hospital. She waited till the night shift nurse was sleepy and snuck out of the hospital with her baby. She begged bus fare to Klong Toey and the sacred grove. Promised herself that, if she ever had some money, she would come back and get Kaewalee's birth certificate. That's what she told the police when they found the drugs in her dirty clothes basket. But they said that didn't count.

Worse, the hospital had wanted a name. A name for her baby girl. Momma didn't quite understand all the legality of registered names. She needed to consult with local soothsayers and ancient ladies in the neighborhood before giving her child a name. How could she decide right there on the spot in the hospital? She didn't have that much schooling and needed to consult. What year of the religious cycle, what lunar month, what day of the week according to the waning and waxing of the moon? All these things are totally important in choosing a name.

Without consulting, they'd think she had no ethics, didn't know her traditions and customs and religion. If she decided a name on her own, maybe the spirits would not be pleased and her baby would not be blessed and protected from evil.

Hospitals function by modern rules, so as is their custom they registered the baby's name as Bua (beautiful lotus blossom), as they name every girl child born there who has not been given a name, plus her father's family name. They need it for their records.

That, as far as we know, was the first and last time anyone even suspected her name was Bua. It simply slipped off the charts. How did her mom choose Kaewalee? It means "woman seeking truth and knowledge." We don't know any more than that.

Mom's in prison for a long time to come. It would be totally bad form to ask her about any special meaning in the name of her daughter who has died. Most likely Momma had consulted with a monk at the temple who looked into the books according to the lunar calendar.

To Momma she was simply Kaew. Easy to say. Easy to remember. Her birth name, Bua Chareonsuk, only became important when she got sick. Who would pay the hospital bills?

She was really sick, even from the beginning. Died in three weeks. At the first hospital, the local quack gave her paracetamol to reduce her stomach pain—she was in agony. Told her to come back in five days. That went on for half a day, till we got her to a proper hospital.

Was it too late? Yes, but it was too late from the moment she got sick. Cancer. No hope.

The hospital said we needed to give her one last chance. Dialysis. Needed money up front. She had no papers. The name we gave was not in the records. So off to see Momma in the slammer. She was the only one who might remember her daughter's real name. Then into the big computer, where her official name was found. Government paid the bills.

We told Momma she was dying and wouldn't make it till the end of the month, and that her only daughter asked for her each day, and in the dark hours of the night before dawn. And to Kaewalee we could only say, your mom loves you more than you can dream of.

Her mom said, "When she dies, please do not phone. Don't ask a guard to bring me the news. Write me a letter with nice pretty handwriting. When I try hard, I can read the words. And by the time the letter arrives, you will have prayed for her at the temple and her spirit will be safe.

"Also when you see Uncle, the junk man, tell him I'm sorry for all the bad words I ever said to him. Please ask him to buy some candles. Light them for Kaewalee. Especially at night ... so that if her spirit wanders, she might see the candle light and find her way home."

# Leader of the Five Kiosk Workforce

**M**s. Kanokthip is president and pioneer/founder of the Klong Toey Slum Chapter of the Physically Handicapped (the Chapter)—that is, the Five Kiosk Workforce. At thirty-eight years of age, she's tough in many ways but very fragile in others. Never went to school. One leg gone from bone cancer years ago. Just recently her husband, while working as an assistant bartender, began a relationship with a short-time girl from a remote province who hires herself out of the bar, and he left Kanokthip. One other thing: Thip is four months pregnant.

Pregnant Thip may be going through a bad patch, but she's a Klong Toey woman. Chances are she'll come out of it with only a few new emotional scars. She lives with her mom and ten-year-old daughter in the house her mom and dad homesteaded in Lock 1 in the Klong Toey slum almost thirty years ago.

Now Ms. Kanokthip and her Chapter control and manage the five kiosks on the main road running through the slum. They hold monthly meetings and make themselves known in the community. They have pride in what they do. Earning respectable livelihoods, they see themselves as first-class (no longer second-class) citizens. True, the sales of soft drinks and power drinks have plummeted since the drug wars started and killed off their night trade. But they keep trying.

These are fragile moments in Klong Toey society, where the most common New Year's blessing seems to be "May you be money rich." Where interest rates are two percent per day. Where perhaps on New Year's day a money lender in a weak moment of largesse might say you don't have to pay interest today on your loan—but probably not. Where the respect you receive and the *wai* you are greeted with are based on money and power, not age or merit.

Folks don't wai Ms. Kanokthip very often. It's not terribly fashionable to wai the crippled poor. Plus the fact that Ms. Kanokthip is from one of those large old Klong Toey families that neighbors know only by first names. And even if they did know her last name, it wouldn't be an impressive one, at least not in a money-rich way.

To say that the opinion of others—what they say or don't say about you—is not important, that's garbage. It hurts when people ignore you. And that's what makes Ms. Kanokthip and her Chapter so very important and so very fragile. Important because their Chapter brings pride and self-respect to the handicapped of Klong Toey and all other slums. They refuse to be ignored. And fragile because it's next to impossible to survive economically on their five donated kiosks.

But they refuse to give up. The personal struggle to get out of bed in the morning, dress, struggle into their wheelchairs, living not in handicap-friendly homes but in Klong Toey shacks. They negotiate inhospitable streets and lanes and broken sidewalks, hand-pushing their wheelchairs every morning to get to work, put in twelve hours and make just enough profit to restock supplies for the next day—day after day.

Economics aside, Ms. Thip and her pioneering Chapter have made a quantum leap forward and are moving at warp speed. It takes great courage to make their own way in the slums and say, "Hey, look at us, Klong Toey. We belong here. We can't read or write, and we can't walk, but we are Klong Toey."

You might wonder how they can operate five kiosks if they are illiterate. But they can sign their names and they can count in every direction. Ms. Kanokthip learned how to count watching neighborhood women playing cards.

As always, though, it's a fragile situation. With a wobbly government-issued wheelchair, bent crutches, no additional household income, no husband, no money in the bank and no schooling, Ms. Thip is trying to make it on her own in her own way. To do that honestly—without selling drugs or the Three K glue in the green cans or the throwaway cigarette lighters that you sniff the gas from—that's extremely fragile. Meanwhile she is raising a daughter who is near the top of her class in school and aspires to be a classical Thai dancer, and she's determined to give her second child a better future.

Fortunately Ms. Kanokthip knows how to sell. As a child she always stayed at home with her mom, who sold cigarettes one or two at a time, occasionally a full pack. Sold locally made booze too, by the shot glass. Stuff that escaped the eye of the taxman.

Mom never sold food because her eleven children, including Thip, who was number five, would eat all the food before she could sell it. Mom never went to school, but she could count. Seems all slum moms know how to count.

Thip remembers her dad fondly. He would gently pick her up every morning and place her in her wheelchair before he went off to the port to look for day labor, which usually involved carrying hundred-kilogram rice sacks up and down gangplanks. He told her many times, "Thip, my beloved, special daughter, never give up hope. Never stop trying." She listened.

It couldn't have been easy to believe her dad. Imagine if, ever since you could remember, it was drilled into you daily that your ailments made you second-class and that it was your own fault, probably because of sins you committed in a previous lifetime. Brainwashed in this way, you become, you remain, always fragile.

It's surely worse for Thip since her husband walked. Back when she was twenty-six, no one had ever told her she was pretty, so she was beguiled by a guy with a sweet mouth, as we say in Thai. She got pregnant, her dad had a conversation with the guy, and he stayed. Later her husband learned how to be an assistant bartender and left her. But life goes on.

Current matters in the slums aren't helping business at all. Since the drug wars started, kiosk sales are way down. No one is around after dark to buy anything. People are afraid of strangers riding by on motorcycles. Mostly they're afraid of the strangers' guns. So when the kiosks are able to stay open twelve hours a day, they average only 150 baht total sales, and the costs have to come out of that. It's pretty thin, fragile. Economically it's the pits.

Yet somehow, fragile or not, Thip and her Five Kiosk Workforce are the strength of the new Klong Toey. They are more than pioneers; they are heroes. How does that story line from the TV show go? Something like ... "they dream and go where no one else has ever dared to go." We, you and I, we the children born of lesser gods, cannot afford to lose them.

It's a sacred place, Klong Toey. (It means "Canal of the Pandanus Leaves.") It's a place where Ms. Kanokthip on

89

her wobbly wheelchair and her bent crutches cannot only survive but even prosper, albeit in a humble Klong Toey way. If you're passing by, stop and buy a soft drink. And if you like, please do wish her and her Chapter a happy and prosperous New Year.

# The Long Road to Mercy

**M**other Gung says her own mother used to tell her, "Daughter, you were born just after sunset in the Year of the Tiger—that time of day when Mother Tiger is hungry and going out to look for food for her babies. Sometimes you find food, sometimes you don't. There will be tough times." And her mom was right, as mothers usually are.

This past month Mother Gung was in the afternoon fresh market, pushing the cart carrying her mob of four (her tiger cubs, as she calls them), warning them not to stray from the cart and run around, as three-year-old kids like to do. Mother Gung was on a mission to buy red chilies, the hottest she could find.

In this same market was an old fortune-teller, down on his luck—not begging, of course, as fortune-tellers consider that below their station—but desperately looking for folks who might want their fortunes told. He told Mother Gung he would "take a reading" from an old tree near the market, a tree well-known for giving winning lottery numbers, but also known for being quite moody and at times arbitrary—meaning it also gives non-winning numbers. He would do this for Mother Gung for only the price of a bowl of noodles. So it was agreed.

The fortune-teller said the tree told him that in this Year of the Black Water Dragon there would be no conflict in the cosmic elements for Mother Gung and her children. Nodding his head wisely, he continued with the observation, "Dragons are water creatures, and you, Tiger Mother Gung, are a land creature. Seldom do dragons and tigers cross paths. He cautioned her to "be careful when giving the children a bath. Don't talk about dragons near the water, and be sure to towel the children properly, with no splashing around."

Mother Gung is the seventh of eight children and came to Bangkok from the Northeast when she was seven. Dad, a harsh man, felt she couldn't watch and control their water buffalo, or climb on its back to ride it, being as she hobbled and couldn't really walk. Best to send her off to Bangkok, to clean and sweep her sister's house.

Mom, pregnant with her eighth child, combed her daughter's hair, making the part in the middle and straight, gave her a hug and walked away, not wanting daughter Gung to see her tears. She thought she would never see her crippled favorite daughter again. She was trying not to cry, afraid somehow that the baby in her tummy would feel her sadness and be born sad. So she whispered the words of an old love song, "Somehow, we will meet again, in a happier place, happier times."

They dressed her in her school uniform and put her on the overnight bus alone. No suitcase, no toothbrush and just a torn-away piece from an old rag blanket to cover her shoulders.

Mother Gung had had "schooling"—first and second grade. She had begged her dad for more. He told her: "Daughter, I let you have your way. You and your mother. Even against my better judgment, you got your reading and writing. It cost me five baht a day for you, and frankly, you're a girl, crippled, and you simply aren't worth it."

As she remembers, her second grade teacher came to their house, also pleading her case: "School is her only chance. She's a smart kid. I'll buy her a new school uniform." Dad didn't put much stock in teachers who weren't from the village and didn't know much about water buffalos. Even worse, the teacher hailed from somewhere down around Bangkok. That ended that. Mom cried. Dad said, "You've got other kids."

On the overnight bus, she sat up by the driver, as her mother had told her to, though she was probably safe anyway. Crippled seven-year-old girls, even with their hair combed properly and parted in the middle, don't score high on the "Let's grab a kid and sell her" scale.

The older sister was supposed to meet the bus, but she overslept. Some "john" had kept her busy till almost dawn. Gung hobbled off the bus, recognizing no one, and sat on the floor of the bus terminal for several hours. She wet and soiled herself, as she didn't dare ask anyone where to go to the toilet. Plus Mom had told her not to talk to anyone.

The first thing her older sister said was, "You stink. Shame on you!"

The older sister was tall, svelte, too popular. Certainly too busy to care for her two babies, whom she bottle-fed lest nursing warp her figure. Besides, it was best no one knew. Bad for business. Crippled baby sister Gung was the perfect solution. Like a servant, but better even, as she didn't have to pay her. Just feed her and give her a place to sleep.

Years passed, and Mother Gung met a man, a factory worker, who spoke nicely to her and stole her heart. He loved his crippled bride and even asked proper permission from her family. But the family was absolutely against the wedding and refused to meet the groom. The situation was this: Gung's family owned some farmland and figured that if

93

Gung married and then something happened, her husband would inherit the land.

But Gung decided she could find happiness living in a rented shack with a man who worked in a factory—a man who spoke nicely to her, didn't drink, didn't even know how to gamble, gave her his pay, even washed her clothes for her. They saved and bought a small TV, and Gung had an old radio for listening to music. They loved each other dearly. He'd always wanted children, but somehow that didn't happen. His only weakness was that he did tend to wander a bit. Three years later, he suddenly fell sick with the virus and died.

She stayed in their rented shack after he died. The landlady said she could stay free for a while and just pay the water and the electricity.

She began spending her mornings in nearby Lumpini Park, usually getting there before dawn, where she met and became friends with the "Lumpini Park girls"—the women who stand outside on the street beside the park in the early mornings before daybreak, seeking customers. That's where she was given her nickname. They affectionately called her Mother Gung. She'd sit at the bus stop and comb their hair, making it neat and pretty like her mother used to do for her.

Eventually she realized she had that virus too, so she decided to end it all. She pawned the TV, the radio and the gold ring her husband had given her, thanked the kindly landlady and gave her money and pawn tickets to her new friends, the Lumpini Park girls. They asked her why she was saying goodbye, so she told them. They held her, cried with her and wouldn't let her harm herself. They told her to sleep in the park and they'd come as they always did, tomorrow morning before first light to see her then.

A brother of one of the girls had died here at the Mercy Centre. So the next morning the girls gave her bus fare and directions. Then they hurried to stand street-side under their umbrellas. Business is slow on rainy days, and they didn't want to miss a customer.

She came to us at first light, hobbling up the steps, asking if she could stay a while. Months later, she said she had promised the Lumpini Park girls who had saved her life she would someday go back, comb their hair prettily, parted in the middle, and they would all have a party. Just them, no customers allowed.

Here at Mercy, she's Mother Gung. Our children collect fallen flowers for her on their way home from preschool. They're happy—three years old in school with a nice teacher and a mother who seldom scolds you and buys you ice cream.

Mother Gung teaches them a lot. Like how to remember the smells of flowers, leaves and plants that you can eat when you're hungry—a skill that lasts a lifetime. And of course, those fire-hot red chili peppers.

After her husband had died, she had taken blood tests at the hospital. The doctor had asked her, "Do you know?" The hurt was so great, she couldn't bear it. So to forget the pain, she had started to eat the hottest peppers in the land.

Mother Gung takes the antivirals twice a day, together with her four children. They take their pills together, so it's a fun game.

What are the secret ingredients of a Mother Gung? Maybe we adults need a secret decoding ring to understand. But the children? They know. Kids know everything.

She can't walk through walls, run fast or leap over tall buildings; in fact she can only hobble. So the kids help her along. They walk together.

When the virus hits them hard, they're off to the hospital. Hospitals have scary sounds in the night. Mother Gung, born in the Year of the Tiger just after sunset, sleeps on the floor next to their bed—tiger-strong against the orcs and trolls and goblins and other creatures of the night who might lurk under the bed. Then when they're sound asleep, even though it's kind of against the rules, she curls up on the bed next to them, whispering in their ears that she loves them and so do their guardian angels.

The kids say she's powerful that way. Especially the next morning, when she buys them ice cream.

# The Warning of the Jing-Jok

On an evening some time ago, as young Yorsaeng left her home in Isan to catch the overnight bus to Bangkok, a *jing-jok* (small house lizard) made its "tak-tak" sound at her. Her momma shuddered. "Girl, that creature is warning you. Make a tak-tak sound back to thank the jing-jok, and change your clothes so the naughty mischievous spirits won't recognize you."

But Yorsaeng only laughed. Her name means something like "the beauty of a temple with a grove of sacred trees under a Northeast pre-dawn sky." And she's a star. No doubt about it. That's a short step below heroine.

Stars are tough survivors with a beauty about them. Also warts, wrinkles thrown in, along with mud from the rice fields between their toes.

She was the baby of the family, the ninth child. Attended the village school and worked the fields with Momma and the family. Daddy died when she was five. She was twelve that night she shrugged off the jing-jok's forewarning and climbed on the bus to Bangkok to live with an older sister and work in her noodle shop.

Bangkok started off ugly. Snotty Bangkok teen girls looked down their noses at her shabby clothes and smirked, insinuating they could not understand her "country" accent.

Washing dishes and helping Big Sister sell noodles in the daytime, she attended adult education classes in the evenings and on weekends. After she graduated from the equivalency high school, she applied for, and got, a job as a cosmetics salesgirl. She was strikingly attractive when they dolled her up with their fancy makeup. Big Sister said the lipstick and rouge made her look like someone she didn't want to be. If people in the village saw her, they would surely get the wrong idea.

Like the warning of the jing-jok.

After her three-month probation the department store people assigned her to sell cosmetics to small-town girls in one of their upcountry stores. Her rural accent would be a benefit there, they thought. She'd be a star.

There she met her first husband, also a farm boy. Armed with a high school education, he'd gotten hired as a salesman at a low salary, plus commission. The more you sell, the more you make.

It took a few months till he sweet-talked her into having a baby. She moved in with him in a rented room just a ten-minute walk from the department store. He didn't tell her his two friends from the village already lived there with him. It was a bit crowded. Common stinky toilets. One for girls and one for boys. A single water tap outside, and you couldn't drink the water.

She was twenty-one when she gave birth to a beautiful baby girl. But you never call your newborn beautiful or handsome, lest those naughty mischievous spirits hear you and steal the baby or make the child sick. So you trick them by talking loudly to the baby (so the spirits can hear you) and calling her "Piggy" or "Puppy" or "Kitty Kat" or "Sparrow."

The big problem was her husband. His money went for karaoke, pubs, tips for pretty waitresses and betting on the weekly boxing matches.

His salary was for him alone. Her salary was for food and the baby and rent. They argued at first. Then one fine morning, looking at a silent jing-jok on the wall of their shack and still nursing her baby, Yorsaeng "had a long talk with herself." She left that evening as soon as he had gone out, one more time, with his village mates and a couple of girlfriends—"cousins," they said.

As she closed the door behind her and threw the keys in a mud puddle, she heard the tak-tak from another tiny jing-jok. This time she listened, and she whispered "tak-tak" back to thank the creature for its warning. She added, "Be well! Find some squishy bugs." She caught the evening bus to her momma's farm.

She never saw her first husband again. Said that if she did, she'd cut his heart out with a dull knife. She stayed with Momma four years, working the fields, caring for her daughter. Momma had always said to her nine children, "Never give up, never look back."

When Yorsaeng's daughter was starting kindergarten, Big Sister asked her if she wanted to come back to Bangkok. She always needed help in her noodle shop.

Yorsaeng kissed away the tears of her first-born. "Momma will come back for you. We'll be a family. You be a good girl and look after Grandma."

Back in Bangkok Yorsaeng would get up first, to go to the fresh market each morning at 3:30 a.m. That's where she met the three-wheel taxi driver man. A monster of a man. Bearded. You just knew he could wrestle a water buffalo and win.

He took a liking to Yorsaeng. When she asked about his past, where he came from, he just looked at her and silently shook his head. But he never missed—was there each morning as she came out the door of her sister's shack to drive her to market in the tuk-tuk that he owned himself.

She gave him two sons. Masters Awt and Amh. Both Northeast strong and wiry like Momma, and growing up to be huge like Dad.

Shortly before Awt was born, Yorsaeng went back to Momma and gave birth to her first son at home. Amh was born in Bangkok, at a government hospital.

That's where she found out her monster tuk-tuk driver husband had given her AIDS, and her first son and now this one had both been born with it too. He swore that he never knew. But blood tests can't be wrong. He'd got the virus somewhere before he met her.

They stayed together, both still healthy, and raised their sons. She loved and forgave her tuk-tuk driver husband—fed him, bedded him, cared for him. He was still strong as the strongest water buffalo and still took her to the fresh market each morning before he drove off looking for customers.

She got deathly sick five years later. Somewhere she'd heard about the Mercy Centre, and her husband took her and the boys there in his tuk-tuk. In bed for a year and a half, she eventually recovered.

And her tuk-tuk driver husband? There was an accident and someone died. With his past police record, he knew—jail for a long time. So he drove all night, moved in with relatives in a distant provincial town.

Then Yorsaeng heard that he had been "meandering," and she was not pleased.

She'd always cut her husband's hair to save money. As a good and pious Thai wife, she'd saved his hair clippings and put them on a banana leaf in water with joss sticks and candles, to ask the Lady of the Waters to protect her husband and keep him from sickness and pain.

But now she gathered the clippings and threw them all out on the street. Watched a stray mongrel dog come, sniff and then do his business there. She took no pleasure in that. Said watching the actions of that dog broke her heart.

After a year and a half in bed, she rented a one-room shack in Klong Toey for herself and her two sons. Recovered for a while, as much as anyone ever does from AIDS. And got her boys back in school again, taking their antiviral meds twice daily.

We needed a star on our AIDS Visiting Team. Yorsaeng qualified perfectly. Only an AIDS person really understands. She'd visit the AIDS sick through the city's slums, encourage them and tell them that after AIDS, life still goes on.

But being alone isn't that much fun. And the slums of Klong Toey are not totally cool for a single woman living in a rented shack, even with two young sons. That's where she met her third husband. He found her. He was renting a shack next to hers. He's a welder in a small ironworks shop here in the slums. She didn't tell him she had AIDS, and he didn't ask.

After a few months they moved in together, "to save rent money." She agreed to take him in, but first she had to ask her sons. They agreed, begrudgingly. Theirs was the joy of earth and sky, for a few months.

Then he noticed that she and the boys regularly took pills, twice a day. He asked why they needed to eat meds. She told him she and the boys had the "I'm allergic disease."

He didn't talk to her for two weeks. Then she asked him, "What now?" He agreed to stay. It worked for a while, till he started drinking. Yorsaeng said, "I'm not going through this again. He will not hurt me and my boys. And I don't want my daughter to know her momma is living with a drunk."

It was like the warning of the jing-jok all over again. Then he started mixing the *ya ba* with his booze. He was making four hundred baht a day. True, the booze was cheap, but the pills, at two hundred baht a pill, two, three pills a day—you work out the math.

She thought of mixing his booze with rat poison or insecticide, but she didn't want to commit a sin. Plus, if she went to prison, her boys would be all alone, and she had promised her daughter that Momma would come back someday.

She began smoking drugs herself. Inhaling is a better word. Maybe just to get even with him. Didn't really know why.

Then one day he said in a joking way that, "ha-ha-ha," maybe he'd let the boys inhale the meth, just for fun, and also her now teenage daughter, who'd come to live with them too. She grabbed a rather unsanitary knife she used to clean fish and threw him out of the shack.

Then she stopped the meth. Just plain stopped. We often think that our love for our children is what saves them, but it can also be true that it's the children's love that saves us.

Yorsaeng's three children took clippings of their own hair and fingernails, and hers, and placed them on the waters in a banana leaf with the joss sticks and candles, asking the Lady of the Waters for a blessing. They hugged her, and her daughter said, "Momma, we're together as a family. We promise you, Momma, no matter what, we'll always take care of you and love you."

The star on our AIDS Visiting Team is back, and now at long last, nowhere can she hear the tak-tak sound of the jing-jok.

# The Old Man and the Sea, and His Granddaughter

It's true. The kids do swim to school, or wade in water up to their neck, when the tides are in. And they love it. Stilt houses on the shore have no connecting bridge, so they swim the fifty meters—clothes and books held dry above their heads with one hand.

Great fun for seven-year-old Miss Jhin and the other children. Not every day, but according to the tides. And cameras. The tide had gone down and a boat arrived from the mainland with the camera lady—not the regular morning boat bringing the teachers and fresh food to cook for the school breakfast and midday meals.

Miss Jhin's favorite teacher, the one she trusted the most, Ms. Phrong, introduced her kindergarten class to the camera lady from the government census office. Miss Jhin pulled her shirt over her face: "No Way! No pictures! I don't trust anybody that much!" She was absolutely certain—no doubt, for sure—that she'd be captured in the camera and would not be able to get out. She didn't know why or how, but she just knew. Just like the television—how did they get out of the picture? But she suggested to the camera lady that she take not just one but several pictures of her four-year-old brother. She didn't dare giggle as she told her this wonderful idea.

# The Old Man and the Sea, and His Granddaughter

Miss Jhin was speaking mostly in Thai but switched over to her native Moken tongue when she couldn't think of the Thai words. Her island is Koh Lao, thirty minutes away by the fast long-tail boats the sea gypsies use off the Ranong Wharf in southwest Thailand. That's home now, on the land; no longer does she live in a boat on the sea.

Miss Jhin was born on the high seas in a traditional Moken boat in the traditional way. She was born with the spirits of the seas protecting her. She is a Thai-born Moken sea gypsy; she doesn't have full Thai citizenship, but she is "recognized."

She cannot leave Ranong province without permission, but citizenship will come in time. And right now she's finishing a full year of kindergarten. She can read and write Thai and do her sums and count in Moken, Thai and English.

Miss Jhin and her family are caught in a time warp. Nowadays, the big commercial boats scour the waters with nets. The fish are no longer that plentiful. The Moken fishermen get the leftovers. Faced with starvation, they must work as hired hands. Their knowledge of Thai is weak and their Moken language is only spoken, not written. They have no words for land ownership. Their language is of the seas and the tides and the movement of the fish. Citizenship documents for them are just the beginning. They have no recourse against the "land folk."

She lives with her grandfather, whom she calls Uncle Sri-dhit. He walks with her each morning to the kindergarten when they don't have to swim and tells her about turtles and how they are sacred. Moken sea gypsy belief holds that the turtle is the most sacred of all living creatures, equal to humans. She once asked him why and he told her, "It just is." Uncle Sri-dhit is their headman on Koh Lao. His face embodies five hundred ocean squalls and uncountable dawns and sunsets on the water. It features pain lines of unbelievable hardship and the human damage of thirty years of freestyle deep ocean diving.

He no longer takes his crew to sea. The recent death of his only son broke his spirit. His son was paralyzed by the bends. It took three years for the condition to kill him. They buried him facing east in a shallow grave in the mangroves on a nearby island. Twice a week, at school, Uncle Sri-dhit leads the prayers in Moken for the spirits of the seas to protect them all each day. Then it's story time. He tells them of days gone by, of their culture and customs.

Memories are of the seas—the men diving, freestyle. A long rope with one end tied to the boat has a wicker basket at the other end to collect sea cucumbers. A long garden hose is wrapped around the diver's waist for breathing. It is connected to an old-fashioned bicycle pump manually operated by a man in the middle of the Moken boat. The middle of the boat, where life takes place.

Even today an "agent" will sometimes come along and ask them to do some diving, no questions asked. Whatever the divers find the agent will pay for, but if the Moken get caught by the officials from the neighboring country, the agent will accept no responsibility.

Sea cucumbers are of huge value in Hong Kong, Singapore and Bangkok, and shells that sing in your ears can always be sold. Uncle Sri-dhit used to make his own depth charges. He is a legend. The agent would furnish the material: gunpowder, an explosive cap, fertilizer and diesel fuel.

He tells these stories to camera-shy Miss Jhin and her kindergarten class with great sadness. The proud Moken people—protectors of the seas and respecters of the sea spirits—are reduced to setting dynamite depth charges that destroy the very sea that protects them.

# The Old Man and the Sea, and His Granddaughter

Uncle Sri-dhit lived for more than twenty years with his family on his boat. During storms they would find anchorage at the nearest shore. But they are no longer welcome at many places along the shore, and diving is not allowed. Many Moken men have been sent to prison work camps. Thai territorial waters are a safe haven, but to survive day by day, they must move onshore to find work.

Uncle Sri-dhit tells how, long ago, his parents told him a story. When he was being born, a turtle came up to the boat and stayed with them, swimming along until after he was born. Now Uncle Sri-dhit suffers the ignominy of living in a shack on the shore. He has had to sell his boat. But his real home is still on the sea. There his spirit is free.

His granddaughter usually sits in the front of the class in their kindergarten shack to listen to Uncle's stories. She tells everyone she is now healthy and will soon no longer be seven, but eight! Sturdy as a half-grown turtle. We gave anti-worm medicine to Miss Jhin and ninety-eight other children on the island. But Miss Jhin was the only child brave enough to pull the half-meter-long tapeworm out of her mouth all by herself and hit it with a broken cockle shell. Now that the tapeworms don't eat half the food, these kids gain a kilo a month and more. And Miss Jhin is a three-helpings-a-meal type of girl. She has the balance of a ballerina—learned from climbing around the boat. Her teacher calls her a graceful turtle in the water and a young mountain goat on land.

Pretty. Not movie star pretty, but wild-like-the-seas pretty. Like a boat-born kid should be. She speaks Moken and Thai pretty well, and Uncle Sri-dhit is now teaching her all the Moken words for sickness and health and the body. She wants to grow up to be a medical doctor.

Conceived at sea, Miss Jhin was the last child born on Uncle Sri-dhit's boat, one of the older-type boats lashed together with strong hemp rope to withstand the violent storms of the Andaman Sea. Still had the stump of the mast in the middle they used to use for wind sails before the long-tail engines.

Seven years ago, while the family still lived on the boat and a couple of days before baby Jhin's birth, they netted some fish; met some Moken "shirt-tail" relatives from another island and bartered for smuggled fuel, rice and cooking oil; then stopped at Koh Lao to ask Ms. Lai Yah if she would travel with them to assist with the birth. She's the famous Moken midwife of the islands—delivered more than one hundred children, many of them at sea. Baby Jhin's mother wanted the birth to take place at sea, felt that that way, the spirits of the sea would always be with her baby, watching and keeping guard. Miss Jhin was also born with the full moon. A good time to be born.

For folks living on the sea the things that matter are the tides, the waning and waxing of the moon and the full moon, the winds and coming storms, the color of the sky at sunrise and sunset, and the movements of the fish. Essential. But days of the week, no. There are no words for the days of the week in the Moken language used on the island, or for months of the year.

Not long after she was born, baby Jhin's father died of the bends diving off the coast of a nearby country. At the time he had joined another Moken boat. "They" caught the whole crew of seven men and confiscated the boat. Her father, already sick from being dragged up too fast from twenty-five meters deep in the sea, died quickly in a prison work camp. Not that medicines would have saved his life, but there was nothing "available for prisoners."

So then her widowed mom had no one to go to sea for her and bring home money from fishing and diving. She was literally starving, so no breast milk for her baby. To survive she came to live on Koh Lao with Uncle Sri-dhit.

# The Old Man and the Sea, and His Granddaughter

He doesn't go to sea anymore because someone needs to be on the island with the sixty families who live there. But his fame as a diver and maker of water bombs is legendary. Been diving without equipment since he was nine. No earplugs, no flippers, just a mask with the garden hose connected. Just you yourself. Down to twenty-five meters.

He prefers to speak Moken. It's an ancient tongue, not much known in these parts now. True, he speaks the five languages of the area. Enough to get by, to tell the young ones what they need to know about the sea.

He loves telling the children his stories of days gone by. To keep alive their customs and traditions and beliefs—speaking in their ancient language. And he loves to watch Miss Jhin study and play, graceful as a half-grown turtle swimming in the sea, and agile as a young mountain goat on land. She loves school and is full of life and joy and dreams. She wants to be a doctor and to get a boat just like the one she was born on and care for all the Moken moms and children in the whole ocean. There is hope for tomorrow.

# PART III

Children of Klong Toey

# A Rainy Night in Bangkok

In the end Miss Sao, now fifteen years old, came across Bangkok town with us to try to find out who her parents were so she could get her ID papers. We had the firepower with us—a Klong Toey plainclothes lad and another from Special Branch—just in case. Plus her beloved substitute mom, Teacher, the one who had smuggled her out of the slum that rainy midnight eight years before. Tippy-toed away from the rented shack where Miss Sao lived with her auntie, granny and grandfather—the sex abuser—to escape to safety and freedom.

Teacher had bought a bottle of foreign whiskey—with a higher alcohol content—for Sao's grandfather. It was a high-risk move because liquored-up was when he looked for his granddaughter to come sit on his lap. But it worked. He passed out, totally hammered. She hadn't been back in all the years since. Didn't dare. We didn't dare.

But justice comes in strange packages. Grandfather died, despised and unwanted after three years in a prison cell. The only ones still living in the rented shack were her dad's younger brother and his wife, the auntie who slapped her to stop her crying when grandfather hollered for her to come and give him a hug. Grandmother too had since died. Sao didn't know anything about her mom and dad, not even their names. Was always told they were useless and better off dead. So eventually she stopped asking.

At that time the grandfather was buying secondhand magazines and taking them to the Sanam Luang area to resell them. That's why he wouldn't send her to first grade. Her sitting there begging beside him was a good moneymaker. Unless it rained he usually made his whiskey money. That's when Miss Sao went to her teacher, crying, and asked, "Can I come and live with you?"

Now Sao was fifteen years old and grown up. Not a cowed, abused seven-year-old, who, with no parents and no identity papers, did not exist in the legal world. Even at fifteen she had no ID papers, but there was some hope.

This time it was daylight in the old slum, and she asked to stop at an old neighbor's house on the way to use the bathroom. She was terrified. She led the way. The slum hadn't changed that much in eight years. Teacher beside her, police following quietly, guns hidden. From the neighbor's house they walked straight to the rented shack she had grown up in. Had to stop at half a dozen houses, neighbors remembering her, all telling her how she had grown up and was so pretty, and greeting her teacher. They all knew the story. There are no secrets in the Bangkok slums.

Then came the unpleasantness. Auntie Malai met her at the door. This time Sao didn't cry. Well, not very much anyway. Plus the two lads moved up a bit closer behind her.

"You animal girl! You killed my dad in prison," said the auntie.

It didn't get really ugly. Easily could have, though. Neighbors crowded around. Teacher shouted, screamed at Auntie Malai: "Shame on you! Shame on you!" The Special Branch lad caught Auntie Malai's attention, smiling that particular policeman smile. Then the auntie started bawling.

Mumbled that she didn't think Sao would ever come back again.

But it was awkward. Sao asked, "Why did you let him do those horrible things? Why didn't you protect me?"

And Auntie Malai just looked down. "I never liked you—had to take care of you, and you were such a brat. Besides, these things happen to us women, and you're not even my blood family."

Then she said, I guess by way of compensation: "Your father lived here awhile, but I threw him out. He moved to another slum a couple months ago."

That's how they learned that Sao's father was alive. The Special Branch lad asked what the father's name was and what he looked like. They got directions, didn't bother to say goodbye.

A five-minute walk to an adjacent slum. Of course he wasn't home; he was working. But they exchanged phone numbers with the nice lady in the noodle shop next door. She said Sao could phone him and his employers would call him to the phone. But he phoned Sao first, and Sao said she'd go to see him the next day after school.

She's popular, so she got her sometimes boyfriend and his biggest gangster motorcycle friend to bike her over to meet her dad. He'd dumped her when she was just a year old, so how could she know what he looked like? But now, for the first time in her life, she knew his name, and, as she told us later, when she saw him, she knew.

This is the easy part of the story. Let's do the next part step by step.

That night after Teacher had smuggled Sao out of the slum eight years ago, before dawn some uniforms from the station across town, friendly to the sex-abusing grandfather, came to us looking for Sao and her teacher. They wanted the girl back, or they would bring a charge of kidnapping.

We told them they must go get a woman police officer to question the girl. No men. No guns, no jackboots.

So while they were at the front door, fuming, we frantically called a child-friendly Klong Toey policeman and our lawyer and Teacher to smuggle Miss Sao out the side door to the Klong Toey station, where she gave testimony that she had come to us freely.

We got Miss Sao and Teacher back through the side door just in time, as the other uniforms brought a very gentle, soft-spoken policewoman to speak to Miss Sao. Was she being held against her will? She proudly showed them her document.

That finished that. The grandfather received a fifty-year sentence. The judge was not amused. Continued abuse of a seven-year-old child over a period of two years. Rejecting his role as protector. Forcing her to beg.

Teacher is now happily married, with a child of her own, nicknamed Sao. She is still teaching kindergarten.

Sao has had no legal documents until now. When she came to us, she was already a full year behind in school. She was allowed to study at a local school, but no certificate would be given. Then a sponsor paid tuition to an international school here in Bangkok. By special exception, she could attend classes, but again no diploma could be given. In desperation we sent her to a special school in one of the provinces, where after some years she was recommended for citizenship.

Now, back to the Mercy Centre in Klong Toey.

Sao has met her dad, who told her, "Oh, yes, of course. You were born in Roi Et Provincial Hospital in the Northeast. Yes, of course there is a birth certificate. Of course you are a Thai citizen.

"And my mom?

"I can't remember her real name, but she called herself Jit. We lived together about a year after you were born. Then we split."

"Were you married properly? I mean, with any ceremony?"

"Well, kind of. I went to Roi Et with your mother to visit her parents, to *khaw khama* (ask for forgiveness) after the fact we were living together and to ask for her hand in marriage. About a year after you were born, we came from Roi Et to Bangkok, and I left you with my younger brother and sister-in-law Malai. But just for a while. Till things worked out.

"Then I went south for a few years, worked on some fishing boats. Haven't seen your mom since then. Don't know where she is."

We will look into finding her mom later. One step at a time.

During school vacation, Sao plans to travel with our staff to the Northeast to seek a copy of her birth certificate, after all these years.

I asked her if she wanted to go back to the slum to see her dad. She shook her head no. But she said that he will probably be around, if he gets sick or in trouble, or something.

I asked her if she would help him. She looked at me for a long moment and then said, "Let's wait and see."

# A Star in the Making

Our almost eight-year-old Klong Toey Miss Nong Ming made the Bangkok ten o'clock TV news a couple of nights ago. She shouldn't have, though. In fact, it was "bad form."

True, the camera blurred her face, but (darn it!) for some dumb reason they blurted out her full name. They also showed the place where she and her family were camping out under the tollway, showed her playing with other kids recently off the street at a "family child protection center."

Trafficked at seven-and-a-half years of age, she appeared on the TV pretty much forlorn, hungry, covered in months of grime, but in a clean uniform like everyone else in the place. She said she'd rather wear her Klong Toey street kid clothes, with those worn out flip-flops. But no matter how poor and ragged, even a glance at Miss Nong Ming on the TV screen told you immediately that there is a hidden greatness in this street child. You just know she's going to be a star.

A thug, a criminal, she ain't. A trafficked child she is. Trafficked by her mom and dad. She's Klong Toey's best! Covered with mosquito bites, half a dozen bigger bruises, feet full of cuts and broken toenails. But there's also good news—the medical people say no sexual abuse yet.

A trafficked child, where her whole family—the mom and dad thing—went terribly wrong. Like Miss Nong Ming being the number one money maker in her family instead of being number one in her first-grade class. Mom said you go to school next year. Now you help me. And her dad too hammered all the time to notice.

Also, she's logged kindergarten time in a slum preschool, plus maybe five months of first-grade time in another social welfare home last year.

Mom lied to the officials. Said all was fine. They no longer lived under the tollway. Dad had a job. They'd moved into a house. In all of Miss Nong Ming's life, they had never lived in a house. So Mom's story was all lies.

The officials believed Mom, and she took her daughter home. Arriving in Klong Toey, Mom didn't even give Miss Nong Ming enough time to say hello to her wildly happy stray dog named Dog. Within an hour Mom had dressed her daughter in her Klong Toey clothes, still unwashed after five months. Dog had been sleeping on them every night for a soft bed. Mom sent Miss Nong Ming off with her rag to pander and wash windshields on that tollway exit leading down into the Klong Toey port. Mom was drug hungry and Dad was booze thirsty.

No school for Miss Nong Ming because of a time conflict. School hours cut into her time washing car windshields, begging and selling flower garlands.

Selling a flower garland? Easy. Doing a car windshield? Almost impossible. Touching their car is a huge no-no. Drivers, even men, feel threatened. "Dirty kid. Don't get any closer! Get your dirty hands off my clean car!" The kids say only the kindest of women roll down their windows to speak to them—and give them some baht coins. Their best hope is to find men driving their own cars who are slightly hammered. They give the most money.

# A Star in the Making

Miss Nong Ming? She was a pro—fifty to seventy baht a day. She'd go out at rush hour when the cars were lined up, waiting for the red light to change.

Between rush hours Miss Nong Ming helped Mom sort through garbage bins, collecting secondhand goods like thrown-away cans, plastic and glass bottles, cardboard and scrap metal. At the junk dealers Miss Nong Ming did the horse-trading, as Mom's mind was not always there because of the drugs.

Mom married young to a street boy. No wedding ceremony—that's for rich people. The dowry was just fifty baht as Mom was pregnant. Used goods.

Soon Miss Nong Ming was born. Dad got more into the booze, was a mean drunk and beat Mom up constantly for money for more booze. Mom wasn't skilled at the occasional sex-for-hire business. She was too embarrassed. So she started doing small drug deliveries for a guy near the slaughterhouse part of the slum. She herself became an addict.

Times always change. The guns and motorcycle hit squads started shooting drug folks. The shootings did not stop the drugs in the least, simply caused adjustments. Prices skyrocketed. Everything became much more clandestine. Part-time "occasional" drug runners, especially addicts like Mom, were dropped. Now, only trusted clan members. Appearances are everything, and to the casual observer the problem had gone away.

But Mom's addiction did not go away, and Dad still had the shakes without his booze. The agent told Mom to get lost or her five-year-old daughter might have an accident—even perhaps disappear.

So two steps down the food chain. Mom now used half an amphetamine pill whenever she could find the cash. Before, in the good old days, it was two a day. Same with

Dad. Now he bought his booze "repackaged" at the local shop. Three shots poured into a pocket-sized brown elixir bottle. The "eleven tigers" medicinal powder mixed with rice whiskey. Moonshine, the cheapest in the market.

Miss Nong Ming has never even slept in a house—only a shack. Mom and Dad are total street people. The best they had when Nong Ming was a baby was a small empty sea-land shipping container. Then the owner needed it, so it was back to living under the Klong Toey five-storey walk-up flats. Thrown out of there for littering and making a general mess, they moved under the tollway.

They camped out there, next to one of the large pilings. No roof, cardboard and a couple of large plastic bags, a partially burned mattress thrown out by someone after a fire. Cooking with scrap wood. Toilet? Anywhere and everywhere. Most embarrassing for a four-year-old girl going on five. Buying water occasionally, at five baht per three-gallon tin.

They had a mosquito net, but Nong Ming slept outside the net with her stray dog. The two of them kept each other warm. Now there were no scraps for Dog, but Dog stayed anyway. Roamed during the day but at dark came back to protect Miss Nong Ming. Sleeping outside the mosquito net because Nong Ming was afraid of her dad in his drunken stupor and her mom wouldn't or couldn't protect her.

Miss Nong Ming and Mom collected sellable items, made maybe fifteen to twenty baht in a whole day of scrounging—the exact price of Dad's brown elixir bottle of booze. The equivalent of three shot glasses. Dad? He guarded cars parked in the slum by night. Soon Mom forced Miss Nong Ming to beg from the cars lined up at the red light at the exit ramp. Collected fifty to seventy baht a day. That's what Miss Nong Ming told the TV camera.

She also told the TV camera that she would always give all the money to her dad—but afterwards said "almost." Sometimes, when she was so hungry that she would cry, she would hide seven baht so she could buy instant noodles. Eat them dry out of the package. Not even share them with Dog. She was that hungry.

The authorities grabbed Mom and Dad for vagrancy, but nothing about trafficking their daughter was mentioned. They brought Miss Nong Ming to a respected government shelter, where she sleeps safely, eats regularly, goes to school. With the new law for children, her mom can't just "come and get her and take her home." Her parents must prove they can feed her, that she will go to school. They will not send her to beg or wash windshields during school hours. There will be regular police visits, etc.

And what will become of Dad? His nights guarding parked cars earn him just enough to eat but not much for the "eleven tigers" booze. Certainly not for buying cigarettes by the package. If he smokes, it's the loose tobacco, hand-rolled in newspaper. Thus, he has to make some choices. The police have warned him, no more vagrancy. All of this will be as it will be.

Mom? We've cut a deal with her, and Dad has agreed. We will give her a hot meal each noon. She has to come and must eat here with us, so we're sure she actually eats the food herself. That should suffice as she continues as a bag lady. Another part of the deal is we will rent her a pushcart at five baht a week. Miss Nong Ming, if and when she wants, can live with us, go to school. Mom can see her every day.

As for Miss Nong Ming, she's brilliant. Today at the government home, she's clean, has clothes that fit her properly. The scars and scabs and broken nails have healed. Special shampoo removed the lice. Now she's got enough to eat. It will take her some months to finally believe that she doesn't have to gorge herself at each meal, that her next meal is safe. She loves school. Top scores in mathematics. Slum street kids learn money counting as soon as they can walk. And as I said above, there are flashes of greatness in this child. She will be a star.

She is worried about Dog, though. We checked, and a neighbor lady feeds Dog most days. Dog still roams but wanders back to their abandoned campsite at dusk. Waiting for Miss Nong Ming to come home.

# Slum Boy on the Knife-Edge of Hell

Six years old, calls himself Ohh. Says his momma gave him that name—her only legacy to her only son. He tells how his mom woke him up late that final morning—kissed him, maybe ten-hundred times, crying, hugging him so tight he couldn't breathe, promising she'd come back someday, but now she had to run for her life.

The previous night, Ohh's father, her husband, hadn't had the machete handy, the one he kept in his pickup truck, so he'd used his fists. Bruised, one eye swollen shut, Ohh's momma was absolutely certain that in his next booze- or drug-fueled rage he would kill her.

The reason? She was Burmese without documents and couldn't get a minimum-wage job. She had been fired from her last job a few days before, and they wouldn't pay her any back wages. Her job? Cleaning toilets and garbage cans.

It happens all the time in Bangkok town—hire illegals to work clandestinely for a while; then don't pay them. Just throw them out and tell them that if they squeal, you'll call the cops.

All of that meant no money to buy her husband booze. So he beat her up. Alone, she had no one to help her. Her neighbors were afraid they would be blamed too, you know, for helping an illegal. Any help she might have found was back home on the banks of the Salween River separating Thailand and Burma.

Her husband slept late in the mornings, a combo effect of his nightly drinking and his supposedly staying awake all night as a watchman. Mom tiptoed to where her son was sleeping, woke him, made him promise not to forget her. Then she was gone. Master Ohh thought it was a dream. That is, till his dad woke up. Seeing her clothing was gone, he blamed his son, cuffing him alongside the head. Dad did that a lot.

Jumping ahead in our story… Full plaster-of-paris casts, keeping both legs immovable, were set as high up as they could go to the top of Master Ohh's legs. The leg casts were yellowed, smelly and poop-soiled at the top because little boys have to go rather often, and busy nurses in hospital charity wards sometimes can't keep up. Plus there were only two nice nurses. The others he thought stern. He was too ashamed and embarrassed to call for them to stick a bedpan under his bottom. The old lady in the bed next to him complained all the time about the smell. Told him he was an orphan brat. He didn't know what it meant but figured it wasn't nice. Not something his momma would call him. All he could do was to cry, but that didn't help either; no one noticed. So he learned not to cry.

Spent over a week in the hospital, as the doctors were cautious and afraid of infections from machete wounds—especially afraid of bone infections where his booze-or-drug-crazed father had hacked at his five-year-old son's legs, just above his feet, cutting through bones on the right leg and nearly severing tendons on his left leg.

Here's how he ended up in the casts, according to police reports and social workers. It was early evening. Master Ohh's night watchman father had parked his pickup at the condo where he drank whiskey through his shift till morning. Ever since his common-law wife had bolted, he always took his son with him to work. Dad was afraid that, if left alone, the boy would run away, or worse, play with matches and burn their slum shack down.

So now he took his son with him to his night watchman job. Would leave him in the pickup, hot and stuffy with doors locked and windows closed. Made him pee in a plastic bag. Dad would threaten his son with the machete, said if he made a mess he would chop his legs off. After work, most days, Dad wouldn't let the boy go to kindergarten and wouldn't even let him out of their shack, where he'd lock the door and sleep off the previous night's booze.

It had been two years since his wife had run for her life, leaving her son with the vague hope that she could sneak back some late morning when his dad was dead to the world from his morning coming-home double shot of booze, grab her son and run. But she was probably too terrified.

She never did love Ohh's dad. No, he didn't really buy her, but almost. When she was still in her teens, he'd grabbed her, used her, embarrassed her, then given her a hundred baht as dowry. Any complaints, he'd report her to the authorities. And worse, she was born on the Burmese side of the Salween River but had no Burmese papers either.

One night he drove the pickup to the condo and began his usual drinking. Counting his money, he was short ten baht for his cigarettes for the night—three smokes for ten baht. So he accused his son of stealing the ten baht to play an hour's worth of computer games. Master Ohh bolted, but Dad caught him, held the boy down, sitting on him. Then using his machete, he began to chop his legs just above his feet.

The neighbors said it was horrible. Dad shouting, cursing, the boy screaming in fear and pain. Someone called the police, and for once they answered immediately. It looked like buckets of blood, but Master Ohh's guardian angels were working double and triple overtime. The hacking missed the big arteries; otherwise, Master Ohh would have bled to death on the spot.

I'll tell you part of the ending right now. Ohh laughs and smiles and is a happy kid. The other part of the ending is cool also. But later for that.

Trouble is, putting somebody in the hospital for ten days isn't exactly enough, legal-wise, to be charged with a major felony. You need to put someone in a hospital for fifteen days under existing law. Or the wounds must be considered life threatening. That's what you need to sentence the bad guy for a long time for something like attempted murder. The courts were lenient to the father of the injured child. Perhaps they reasoned that it was only temporary insanity, and time would heal the natural bond. In any case, that didn't happen. But the judge had no way of knowing there was no bond to heal.

After ten days in the hospital charity ward, Master Ohh was released and came to us, stiff-legged in his casts, sprawled in the back seat of what may be the oldest surviving taxicab in Bangkok. The disgruntled driver charged an extra thirty baht because, even keeping the windows open, he was afraid the urine smell would linger in his cab and drive away customers.

Our best house mom, Auntie Whee, and Ms. Dhao from our legal aid team met Master Ohh at the taxi with a wheelchair and a bowl of ice cream. After Ohh gulped down the ice cream, they wheeled him up our ramp to the second floor, where Cookie Crumb James and Superman Awt, plus some other kids of Ohh's age, were waiting to greet him. They presented Ohh with his new school uniform, gave him some books and told him that he was a schoolboy now. Later they put Master Ohh—now in uniform with schoolbooks in hand—in a red toy wagon and pulled him around the playroom. Master Ohh had come home.

Ice cream, school uniforms and a ride in a red toy wagon made all the difference. Plus he'd already met and trusted Ms. Dhao, who had been at the hospital dealing with another child abuse case when Master Ohh was carried into the emergency room. From her daily work in child and family court and police stations, she is a familiar face among the police. She said we could look after the boy if the courts allowed it. He had nowhere else to go.

Auntie Whee, helped by the children, cleaned up Master Ohh real good, getting rid of most of the odor, cutting away the most soiled part of the cast where it came up to his hips. That took care of everything that day except the nightmares in the evening and his midnight screams for help, crying for his momma. Auntie Whee sat him up, held him, cradled him all night that first night, and when dawn came, it was better.

That was six months ago plus a few weeks. Until very recently Master Ohh said he was a five-year-old, even though he was six, because he hadn't yet figured out that once you run out of fingers on one hand, it's totally proper to continue on the other hand. He's getting there, though. Wears his school uniform shirt everywhere. Tells everyone he can read and write his name, almost.

Last week we went through a rough patch. Saturday morning, and Master Ohh was eating second breakfast. Our guards phoned to the second floor. A man outside was demanding to see Master Ohh. A man with nasty manners and nasty language. Master Ohh ran to Auntie Whee, jumping into her arms. Shaking, heart beating, he started to cry softly like a whipped puppy or, in actual truth, like a very real boy who has been terribly wounded and damaged.

Holding him worked; he focused. But then he looked at his legs, said they hurt again, where the machete had chopped him.

His buddies gathered round to defend him. Cookie Crumb James found a vehicle, a fast getaway car, like in the movies. In truth it was a broom handle he could ride Ohh away on. Another buddy, Master Awt, ran and put on his superman cape. One of the girls, Miss Aht, took off the religious medal given to her by her granny and put it around Master Ohh's neck to protect him. He sobbed and gulped and said he wanted to eat ice cream—and with the mention of ice cream, we knew the bad patch would pass.

The nasty man downstairs was the machete-hacker. He'd done his six months in prison. He wanted to see Master Ohh. Said he wanted to *kae khaen* (revenge). He blamed his son, his own flesh and blood, for sending him to prison. We don't believe in revenge. However, we did flag down a child-friendly policeman who happened to be here in Klong Toey. He whispered something to Master Ohh's father. They had a conversation. No one actually heard what was said, but the child-friendly policeman was frowning as only a longtime slum-experienced policeman can frown. Also he kept patting his police pistol and rattling his handcuffs. The nasty machete man walked away quickly.

Master Ohh is safe. He's jumped from first to third kindergarten. He can count on both hands now. He's growing like a weed, so we had to get him a bigger school uniform. Three months now out of his leg casts, he walks better, almost perfectly.

He does his homework together with his buddies, Cookie Crumb James with his magic broom, Master Awt with his superman cape and Miss Aht, who gave him her sacred medal. Their whole gang will begin first grade together in the next school year. Every morning Ohh looks out to the street to see whether his mom is there, having returned for him as she promised.

She hasn't come yet, but we're all sure she will.

# When Flower Girls Grow Up

This one begins rough. And the middle part is rough too. And the ending? Well, I guess you swallow hard through the tears and you shut your eyes tight to squeeze out tears so that you can look up and maybe see a rainbow, and then maybe you cry a bit again, because somehow, for so many of us, way down deep, we want—we demand—more than a rainbow. And that isn't how life works.

This one's about two heroines: Miss Gook Gik and Miss Nong Lek. Their scumbag moms were always lurking in the shadows. The money was never enough for their moms, no matter how much their children scored. The moms' rules were blunt: You girls con money from bar bums so we can play cards. The money, of course, was never enough. Money goes fast in a card game.

It's the same here as anywhere else. They let you win the first few hands. Only in a game of "Let's Pretend" can you find cute, happy heroines. We are taught that proper behavior for seven-year-olds is playing with dolls, hopscotch, jump rope, that they're all whispers and giggles. Not heroine stuff. Life doesn't work that way either.

Miss Gook Gik, thin and willowy, her AIDS temporarily in remission, remarked a while ago, "I earned five hundred baht each night since I was five, and my mom never thanked me once."

Her friend, Miss Nong Lek, was born with a short leg and an accompanying limp. But she never got AIDS, even though she earned less money as a child than her sex worker friends. Her mom used to tell her, "You hustle, girl—errands and drugs if you won't do the other stuff." And so she ran errands every night. Growing up, Nong Lek took countless long walks home alone in the early morning hours back to her Klong Toey shack on the nights she hadn't earned her keep.

Now, over fifteen years later, she still breaks down in tears when she tells you that these walks were agony, but back then she only cried when no one could see or hear her—alone, limping home. No one back then really bothered her, just laughed at her occasionally, called her "gimp." And she walked a lot because, it's true, she was a hustler, but always brought in less cash than the sex workers. Mom and Dad used to take turns beating Nong Lek for her low earnings, but she never gave in. Gook Gik, on the other hand—well, that's how she eventually got AIDS.

Now the girls are young women. Mom visits Gook Gik every other day or so in our AIDS hospice. You might call it a kind-of-sort-of thank-you. But all the visits in the world don't count unless Gook Gik accepts. The forgiveness comes from the offended victim, doesn't it? That's the only way it works—the innocent forgiving the guilty. And that actually seemed to happen this recent Thai New Year, when Gook Gik knelt together with good ol' Mom to make merit, offering alms to the monks. The daughter, seeking a traditional blessing on this sacred day, poured blessed temple water over her mother's hands and feet.

Nong Lek, who is Gook Gik's only thick-and-thin friend, knelt beside her. Her own mom was busy that day.

(One thing you never do is interrupt a card game—not even for a sacred rite.) So Nong Lek came limping alone on Thai New Year to make merit and seek a blessing.

I watched—ashamed for my tears. Slum life here in Klong Toey created these two beautiful young women, and sometimes I see in them and their friendship the heart and soul of Klong Toey.

These two young ladies were among the original Patpong flower girls, selling red roses—always red roses—first on the street outside the bars, then inside. That went on for years. They were born a few days apart. Both their moms fled the hospital, refusing to pay the bills and the accompanying fee for a birth certificate. Without this document the girls could not enter school, so they worked for their moms. Gook Gik's mom eventually went to prison for procurement—a highly publicized event—and while she was in prison, Gook Gik and her two sisters went to work in a bar in Phuket while their brother was being pimped in Chiang Mai. Mom had started them on a path.

Meanwhile, Nong Lek stayed in Klong Toey. While her mother gambled and sold drugs, Nong Lek washed dishes in a street-side noodle shop, sold garlands on street corners— anything, except what Gook Gik was doing. Nong Lek herself finally went to prison in place of her mom for drug possession with intent to sell.

That's how Nong Lek began her formal education—in the juvenile home. She will complete high school in just a few months and become the first in her family ever to graduate. She says she will be a social worker and help other girls.

Today, two years after an accident in Phuket, Gook Gik can walk again, though not too fast or far. She had been bruised up badly when riding sidesaddle on a rented 250 cc with a john. She was spacey on *ya ba* and her john was hammered. He went to heaven that way.

A hospital admitted her into its emergency room after her two sisters, who worked in the same bar, pawned two gold chains for the initial bill. When the hospital wanted to do more tests, the sisters wheeled her out the side door and loaded her onto the next bus back to Bangkok. Bought her two seats and got a friend to shoot her up with a combination of sleeping pills and heroin to make the twelve-hour bus trip back to Bangkok a bit more tolerable.

She phoned Nong Lek to meet her at the Southern Bus Terminal. Her timing was right on. Just a month before to the day, Nong Lek had walked out of the juvenile prison for children, with five years reduced to three plus a few days—finally, a free woman.

Nong Lek had taken the rap for her mom. Sixty-eight pills in full sight when the uniforms walked in. At times it seemed that Nong Lek's mom's rented shack was a veritable pharmacy with a full stock of selected brands on hand that the uniforms like to "make disappear." Literally a minute before the cops' arrival, her mom had spotted the uniforms (her dogs snarled their dog alarm), giving her a few split seconds to stash the rest of the pills and slip out the bedroom window. Nong Lek was sound asleep. She had just come home from working all night washing noodle bowls in the street-side shop and, feeling exhausted, fell right asleep.

As a good daughter, Nong Lek protected her mom. Said they were her pills. Apparently, the day before the bust, her mom, whose tongue was sharp even on good days, had broken the most basic of Klong Toey codes: never curse a neighbor, especially another seller, in front of a crowd. Thus the police were asked to take action.

Five years is pretty much the max for a juvenile. An adult caught with that amount would do double the time. That's for first-time offenders, and Nong Lek's mom is no stranger to police stations. So Nong Lek did the time for her mom.

Nong Lek answered the call from the Southern Bus Terminal and collected her oldest friend. The two of them—Nong Lek still scratching with prison scabies and Gook Gik in a full leg cast—ended up on our doorstep a few days later. That's when Gook Gik first discovered she had TB and AIDS.

Now, two years later, once a month Gook Gik's mom loads her into a rented four-wheel mini Daihatsu—the poor man's taxi. Mom laughs every time they get in, reminding Gook Gik how she was born in one of these Daihatsu taxis on the way to the hospital. Mom was in a card game and had a winning hand that would pay for the taxi ride to the hospital. The pain came, but she had to finish the hand. Mom laughs. Gook Gik winces. Doesn't like to hear the story.

They travel to a nearby hospital for the thirty-baht AIDS antivirals, always using Gook Gik's younger sister's identity card. Gook Gik doesn't look much like the photo of her sister, but a couple of months ago, when questioned, Mom screamed at the top of her lungs: "AIDS! She has AIDS! Give her the medicine or she'll bite you and infect you too."

When Gook Gik was two, her dad died in the hold of a rice barge. Something happened to make the cargo shift, and he was buried in one hundred kilogram sacks of rice. At the Police Hospital they said he died instantly of a broken neck.

Gook Gik's mom asked the *long ju*—the Chinese manager who looks after affairs for the owner—for her husband's pay on the day of the accident. The *long ju* told her, "Sorry, he hadn't worked a full day." And besides, he continued, he himself had paid the pickup driver to take her husband to the hospital. A couple of months later Gook Gik's mom convinced Nong Lek's mom that the two of them should get the *long ju* drunk. Once they got him hammered, they got in several good licks. Twenty-seven stitches in all. (He never reported the incident to the police.)

Nong Lek's dad is twelve years older than her mom and still works heavy manual labor at the port. He's quiet and he doesn't drink, but he has a terrible temper. Though he's been known to beat his wife, he has absolutely nothing of his own. He gives every baht he earns to his wife. It's true, a wrong and a right don't make two rights, but at least there's something there.

From the very beginning it's always been about "following the money." When the kids were still young, the moms took their children to con the bar bums and sell red roses. Guess they had cut some kind of deal: drugs and child sex for wholesale prices on roses—stuff that you really don't want to know about. The kids started selling outside the bars, then inside the bars ... and in Gook Gik's case, eventually, inside a hotel with her mom.

At the hotel there were always two rooms. In one, a customer and one of her children. Or for a huge price, two or three of her children and their friends together. In the other room, always prepaid, sat Mom, usually watching TV soaps or game shows.

So that's the basic story of Nong Lek and Gook Gik and their moms. For Gook Gik her final rainbow isn't far away. It will fade at the Temple by the Bridge. Twenty-three years old now, she will never see twenty-five—the age in Thai custom that decides where the rest of your life will lead. It's called *ben-ja-pate*.

Tear-stained heroines, bruised black-and-blue, these young women are still no less than heroines—heroines perhaps on the backside of its definition. They have lived for years as wounded fauns; they have toughed it through every pawing stranger; and yet they still remain beautiful and without hate, even to this day.

Gook Gik is the elder of the two, and that's important among Thai friends. But in truth she had her *ben-ja-pate*—her deciding year in life—long ago. Nong Lek probably will live to a ripe old age. She's the survivor.

They were together just yesterday here at the Mercy Centre. Nong Lek had just dyed her hair red. Gook Gik had dressed up a bit into something more special than her "just hanging around" clothes. She is in better health these days and out of bed most of the day with only an afternoon nap. And she helps with the other patients when she's in the mood.

On the day of her last visit, Nong Lek had come by to take Gook Gik to the nearby Lotus store. Sitting on a bench at the Mercy Centre, the two friends whispered and giggled together, just as they had so many times and so many years earlier. I sat down and joined in.

One of our nurses warned Gook Gik not to overdo it—she was still weak. She nodded her understanding and the two continued to whisper and giggle.

When the conversation turned to the future, I asked Nong Lek if she would take Gook Gik's place when her dear friend goes away and be her spirit here—in school and everything else in life. She promised—said that she would graduate for both herself and Gook Gik, that she would live the years that Gook Gik will never have, and that she will be Gook Gik's tomorrow and have children and name her first girl Gook Gik and give her all the love the both of them never had.

And when Gook Gik goes, Nong Lek will take her to Wat Sapan, the Temple by the Bridge here in Klong Toey.

Gook Gik won't be going away quite yet. She's not strong and can't work hard, but she's getting rambunctious and has a boyfriend in our AIDS hospice. (He buys her cigarettes.) She feels she will be strong enough in a couple of weeks to make the bus trip to Phuket, where she'll stay awhile with her sisters, hang around the bar and enjoy a last hurrah.

She will come back to us after a few weeks or months in Phuket and then stay with us a while longer.

There is a certain kind of honor in being cremated in Wat Sapan—the Temple by the Bridge. If I were Buddhist, that's where I would want to go. They say the spirits of this temple are very slum-friendly.

Sitting on the bench that day, Gook Gik asked us to spread her ashes in the Chao Phraya River—and we agreed because, really, "Death is a river flowing into an ocean."

# The Pride of Klong Toey

The triplets, all girls, are fourth grade students. Total look-alikes. Same height, same weight. Favorite activities this week are jacks and jump rope. They are the essence of ten-year-old Thai girls—"sugar and spice" plus giggles and more giggles and can't sit still even two seconds.

And secrets. Maybe the best "secret tellers" on this planet. And then they giggle at their secrets, falling all over themselves. Most unladylike!

They sleep with arms and legs sprawling everywhere, their beds pushed together in our girls' dormitory. Their current goal in life is to have as much fun as they possibly can and giggle their way through the day.

Oh, of course, they go to school. Top third of their class. I can't really tell you about their test scores or grades because they constantly switch papers, desks—just for fun. If one of them is sassy, no one knows which one to scold. They get up when they're supposed to, all that stuff, but that's only to have a good time, tell secrets and giggle.

They skip along footpaths, giggle, chirp, chatter. They have signals—really a special world all their own— particularly at secret-telling time, which is pretty much all the time.

It started off so wonderful. Dad, Mom—whose name is Bho—are both high school graduates. Different schools in Klong Toey. Noticed each other in high school, graduated, married at twenty.

When the doctor told Bho she was pregnant with triplets, she came home dreamy-eyed. Bho and the girls' father, Dhey, were still in love, renting a Klong Toey shack near Bho's mom, Granny Praphai and Stepgrandpa. Granny was then still working nights. *Peen rua* we call it in Klong Toey. It means climbing up the backside of a docked ship to offer whatever services and solace any lonely sailors might seek. Cash up front, usually with booze and food and foreign cigarettes to sell later to her neighbors.

When Bho told her mom she was pregnant with triplets, her mom said not to worry. Your momma will be here for you. There's always a ship in port, always one more sailor. Her stepdad promised some of his daily whiskey money. That was before the troubles.

They named their first-born Somruthai (meaning "as wished for" like a beautiful gift sought from the heavens) and nicknamed her Fon (gentle rain). She is delightfully bossy. Their second is Saitara (gentle stream with clear water). Known as Fa (beautiful sky), she is gentle and never argues with her sisters. And their youngest is Wasana (good fortune), and her nickname is Fai (cotton blossom). Wasana giggles the most of all the girls. She was so tiny and fragile at birth that many times Bho thought she was dying.

Recently Dhey lost his job as a shopping mall guard. Says he's put his name in at several places. But just between you and me, that's a long shot. He only got the last job because he used a bogus name. (He's got a record.)

Granny Praphai lives in the back of Klong Toey next to the dead water canal, where the punters raise and train the fighting cocks. Crippled from a stroke for seven years now,

Granny always lies on the floor with the front door open, which doesn't shut anyway, and moans when she needs help to prop herself up in her wheelchair. Beside the shack sits Stepgrandpa's pushcart, rusting amid whiskey bottles. He was a bag man: a collector of bottles, plastic and glass, cardboard, anything. Most of the whiskey bottles there were his. He died a few months ago. The Demon Rum finally got him.

Since the time Granny couldn't climb a ship's gangplank anymore, she has supplemented the family income by playing cards. Never wins big. Neighbors never catch her cheating, although they know she does.

Bho is now thirty-three. Back in the days when the triplets first attended our Mercy Centre preschool, she had money. She'd dress her girls alike, with matching hats and clothes. They were the pride of Klong Toey. Even had a Western-style stroller. When the kids were three, she and Dad would take turns bringing them to preschool each morning. Neat, clean, well-dressed. That first year of preschool, the girls seldom missed a day.

Bho was wearing noticeable gold in those days—"furniture," we call it. But suddenly having furniture comes in the same heartbeat as dealing drugs. It's a sure sign.

Everything went downhill from there. Always does. Soon the gold was gone and Bho was getting irritable. The bad guys won. They got Bho addicted so she would be forced to sell more stuff, and they could then pay her in drugs. Didn't need to give her much cash.

Mean. Ragged. Unraveling. As her daughters began their second year of preschool, Bho went from bad to worse. Then it was all over. Totally fell apart one day when Bho had the kids in their stroller and one cried. When Bho picked the child up, a packet of drugs that she had stashed in her daughter's clothing fell out in front of an undercover cop, who had been watching her for days. Her girls were screaming, hanging on to Bho as the police dragged her away. They had to fetch Granny in her wheelchair to comfort the children and bring them home.

The triplets' dad, Dhey, lingered around for a few weeks and then ran away for some years. With nowhere to go, the triplets moved in with crippled Granny Praphai and Stepgrandpa.

With Bho in prison, on sunshine days here in the slum, with tremendous effort, these four-and-a-half-year-old girls, weighing about fifteen kilos each, would push and shove with Stepgrandpa to get Granny into her wheelchair and then push her through the slum paths, bumps and puddles, as she brought them to our kindergarten. Granny had only one good arm, so sometimes the wheelchair would go in circles. And the girls would cry and cry.

By then Granny had stopped ship visiting, but the triplets depended on her, and they were missing more school days than not. There were rumors about the triplets. "Best give them to social welfare," the neighbors said. "They're like sick kittens."

The next day the neighbors wheeled Granny and the girls to our Mercy Centre. Asked us, could we help? Granny signed. She'd always been proud of her handwriting, but her stroke had ruined that forever, so we had to do a fingerprint too ... just in case. And Granny cried.

The neighbors only got Granny to sign because they were afraid that Stepgrandpa would "rent out" his granddaughters as down payment on a couple of cases of whiskey. Threatened to do so a few times.

So after Granny signed the papers, that very afternoon after school, the triplets moved in with us. For over a year they were under strict medical care. They had been missing a lot of meals.

That was seven years ago. Now Bho has married again. Her new husband drives a garbage truck for the city. Recently, Bho gave up her job collecting bus fares to care for Granny Praphai. She visits our Mercy Centre often to see her daughters. This past week Bho took them to see Granny. The girls asked Bho if they could stay overnight, sleep over just once with their mom, but Bho refused. Maybe the loving hurts too much.

Dad is now back in Klong Toey and visits too. Strangely, he recently began taking home the clothes hamper full of his daughters' dirty school uniforms to wash every week. Said it was something he could do.

But that has now stopped because some bad stuff is driving him bonkers again. Most probably glue mixed with paint thinner. He's spaced out and wild-eyed.

Looking back these seven years, we know Mom and Dad loved their daughters. Maybe Mom and Dad weren't ready, but then life catches all of us off guard, doesn't it?

Mom and Dad come around now on separate days. Their triplets—still the Pride of Klong Toey—are growing up. They know they have a mom and a dad and a sick grandmother whom they visit, and they save their lunch money for Granny so that she has a bit to bet with when she plays cards with her neighbors.

I asked the girls what they want to be. Miss Fon, the oldest, and Miss Fai, the youngest, both want to be doctors—Fon to take care of children when they get sick, Fai to take care of baby birds who fall out of their nests. Miss Fa, the middle child, wants to be a lady soldier. Says she looks pretty in a uniform.

# Mom's Baby Mule

With the sound of that lady judge's voice still ringing in her ears—even after three months in the kids' slammer for girls—Miss Angela came to us here in Klong Toey in a prison van from a Bangkok girls' remand home—middle seat, sandwiched between two custodians.

That lady judge had said: "This is outrageous! Eighteen hundred pills? Lock up this child and throw away the key, to protect her." Then sternly to the arresting officers: "You catch those criminals who used this child. Take her away. Hide her. Protect Her. Educate her as long as you can, at least till she's eighteen. Do whatever you have to do." And she added bitterly: "You tell the mother, if there is ever any buying and selling to do—and I do not want to know about any of it—tell her to sell herself, never her children."

Miss Angela came to us a mess—skinny, lice, dirty fingernails, smelly, scratching herself, runny nose ..."much past smiling." But that was an easy problem to solve—with a huge triple helping of ice cream and cookies and junk food for all the girls, to welcome the new girl, plus a serious "scrub-a-dub" with sweet-smelling soap and this gunk you put in your hair to make the lice go away. New clothes. A promise she could go back to school the very next day.

A phone call to her mom. And most of all, her two best girlfriends in school live here with us. Easy.

That she'd just come from girl's prison? Ho hum! She fitted right in. The girls played rock–paper–scissors to decide where her bed would be and her place at the table. It was that easy. The days turned to weeks, and weeks to months, and months to years. She's one of those "Hey, it's really stupid to try to get into trouble" kids, plus those three months in remand, well ... She says she remembers every minute of those terrible days and nights. Now she's growing up happy. She's in commercial college—grown up, from proper slum girl to proper young woman.

But those three prison months ... Prison girls are cruel to nine-year-olds with brown hair and light skin, *farang*-looking slum girls who have never met their Western dads and wouldn't recognize them on the street. Most of all the girls expressed total prison scorn and disgust for a girl so dumb she didn't know she was carrying drugs. That her mom lied to her—so stupid! Had she been an adult, she'd have been sentenced for life.

And she lived in total fear because some of the older girls wanted to touch her in the night. And when they tried, she would wet the bed and scream, waking up everyone, with everyone cursing her—thus her nickname, Dumb Screaming Farang. Especially the dumb part! So dumb she didn't have a clue about the drugs. They'd tease her that she was a slow-witted water buffalo. Years later at our Mercy Centre she would still sometimes wake up in the night screaming. It took her a while to stop the bed wetting she'd done for self-protection.

The remand home folks had been worried. She was not eating. They phoned us—we know them and have an agreement with the Ministry of Justice. Could we protect a girl from Klong Toey? If she stayed with us, could we keep the bad guys away?

After some horse-trading we paid her bail. Usual bail fee for both children and adults runs at five thousand baht for the first pill and then down to three thousand baht for each additional pill. Nine-year-old Miss Angela had eighteen hundred pills in her knapsack. The court asked us, as a mutual gesture of goodwill, would we post twenty thousand baht, which would be refunded later?

This is how it started. Nine years old. Two older sisters who could have done the drug runs, but Mom didn't trust them. They'd talk, brag, show off, and tell their boyfriends. Maybe borrow a pill or two or three from the stash and sell it themselves for cigarette money. So Angela, who had never been in trouble a day of her life, became Mom's sucker girl.

Mom asked her, very sweetly, to wear this new backpack with her school uniform—to take the Klong Toey ferry across the river and give the backpack to the fat lady. The fat lady would give her a backpack in return that looked just like the one she was carrying. Easy. Mom would buy the ferry ticket.

The scheme worked for a while. Then the undercover police lady noticed. A schoolgirl out of place. An adult buying a ticket for her, then sending her across the river alone. They grabbed Angela and tried to tackle her. Angela bit the police lady and squirmed away.

She ran, screaming for Mom, but Mom was gone. Mom always told her about strangers. Run and scream. Find a lady selling veggies or fish. She will protect you, even if she doesn't know you. Or jump in the river. Scream louder. Don't get caught! Ever.

Of course the police did catch her, and her stash of eighteen hundred pills. That first night in jail they locked her in the adult cell with the women (they had nowhere else to keep her), but the guards made sure the child slept up front, all curled up but with one foot sticking through the bars, next to the cell door, where everyone could see her. They even made jokes, saying her foot was still free.

Plus one of the women, a "card game regular" at the police station, was a next-door slum neighbor. How do you tell a nine-year-old that her mom has used her? Used her bad. Auntie Neighbor Lady held her through the nighttime prisoner noises and groans and shadows till the morning light, when the ghosts and bad spirits crept off to wherever they hang out during the daylight hours.

It would have been Angela's fifth trip across the river. Her mom had agreed with the agents to seven trips to clear all debts. Angela did not see Mom for five years. That's what the judge ordered. Phone calls—well, not often, but OK. But Angela stopped that. Tired of Mom crying over the phone telling her how sorry she was. Mom had lied. Oh how she'd lied! Said that Granny (whom Angela had never met and who, she found out later, had never existed) needed special medicine.

But the loan was real. Mom had borrowed at the normal slum rates of twenty baht interest per day per every one hundred baht. On the payback she'd miscalculated. Forgot to factor in the weather. It was storm season on the high seas, meaning there were few ships in port and thus no sailors or middle-aged lads looking for a midnight massage from a not-so-thin-anymore forty-six-year-old lady with a bit of gray hair plus a few sags and wrinkles. Finding folks who wanted midnight massages was not as easy as in years gone by. Mom simply could not make payments.

The moneylenders smirked. Give us Angela for only three days to cover all debts, plus we'll buy the little darling a new school uniform and a teddy bear. Back to the third grade. No one will ever know the difference. We'll return her safe and sound the day after tomorrow. Mom knew of a slum neighbor girl, Angela's age, who was never heard of again. Such accidents are not that uncommon in Klong Toey, certainly never spoken of, even among closest relatives and friends. No one talks of missing kids. So Mom felt she had no choice.

After Angela was caught, Mom started drinking by the bottle, not the glass. The brokers still wanted their money. Mom paid in dribs and drabs, mostly not even making interest on her debt. But slum women stick together. Finally, the wife of a guy well-known in Klong Toey asked her husband to ask a longtime friendly policeman to please "have a conversation" with those two bad guys.

Angela was with us almost ten years, and this was her home. She grew up here and was known as Ann—everybody's big sister. Always there for her younger sisters, to listen, to help with homework, to hold and to dry tears. Everybody called her Pee Ann (older sister Ann). Without a doubt the most pleasant girl in the house. Above average in her studies.

One day she announced, "I'm ready to go back to my other home." She went back home on her nineteenth birthday. The girls in the house threw a party. Giggles and laughter and tears.

She lives just down the street. A five-minute walk. She continues her studies. That was the agreement. She attends commercial college, almost an honor student in her final year. She stops in to see us now and then, always telling the younger girls they should never, ever carry drugs, not even for their mom.

No serious boyfriends. She likes boys but just isn't ready. She wants to finish school so she can always get a good job, pay her own way. Doesn't want to depend on any man for her living.

The bad guys who had her run drugs? One was shot dead in a card game. The other died of some disease.

As for Pee Ann, all the girls in the house are already planning a big fun party for when she graduates.

# Eight-Year-Old Head of the Family

It's the pits to be hungry when you're eight years old. Even with practice. And Master Moe had lots of practice.

Once again Mom and Dad were doing "government service," as it's called. Not locked up in a cell, per se, but it was suggested to them that they stick around the station for a few days and nights. If they strayed? The evening news would report they were "shot while attempting to escape." Lethal, most serious stuff.

"Government service" also meant eight-year-old Master Moe would again act as head of the household, and seven-year-old cousin Sai as "mom" for the younger three, Master Dhuey, Miss Gig and one-year-old Miss Gook. With Moe and Sai in charge after the early morning raid, that day they didn't go to school. Too shocked. Too hungry. That night the younger three cried for their momma till dawn, and nature took its course with baby Gook doing her baby thing—poop, soaking the bedding, and the place stank with a mighty odor.

Early the next morning Moe and Sai were awake and the younger three asleep when the drug control lads raided their shack again, just as they had the dawn before when they had "invited" Mom and Dad to visit the station.

A neighbor lady, of a betel nut chewing age, didn't like police uniforms. (She still insisted her son had only borrowed the goods found in her house last year.) So she stormed into the shack, berating the drug squad. They ignored her, but she was loud, persistent and nasty, so they joined the shouting contest and screamed at her to get out. That drew a crowd. Nobody in the whole slum neighborhood really liked Moe and Sai's family, but they liked the police even less, just on general principle.

Undeterred by the ruckus, the racket, the children crying and the odor, the police ransacked the shack again. Found a few more pills and some loose change. Not much money, but they took that too. "Sorry, it's evidence!" The children watched in horror as the authorities trashed their shack—their home—tearing it apart. They still talk about that day.

A neighbor lady with a two-table, six-chair, mom-and-pop-style slum eating place told Moe she had some rice she couldn't sell yesterday, but it wasn't spoiled yet. After eating, Moe, carrying baby Gook, and Sai, leading her little brother and sister by the hand, walked over to the police station to see Mom and Dad. But now they were in serious trouble. The Drug Suppression lads had found the other part of the stash of drugs, which came to nearly a hundred pills, but not quite. However, with a bit of "assistance" from the station, the eventual count added up to just over a hundred pills. One hundred is the magic number. Mom and Dad were looking at maybe ten years, maybe a life sentence, with no parole in sight.

Now it was straight to prison. The children arrived just in time to see their folks climb into that black van that says "Police" on the side with the cyclone fencing on the windows, and they all started crying. The van waited, and they took off Mom's handcuffs so she could hug her children, hold them one more time. Dad, no.

It was their last hug for several long years. Their momma's parting words: "Go now, quickly, take everything to the pawnshop."

Sai knew how. She'd gone with Mom before, during some tough times. They'd carted off their rice cooker and fan to hock at the local pawnshop for food money.

A fan and a rice cooker aren't any good without electricity anyway. The mean, nasty neighbor guy next door had cut off their electricity the minute the Drug Suppression team left for the station with Mom and Dad on the back of police motorcycles. Mom and Dad had bought a small, illegal electric meter and doglegged it, slum-style, to the neighbor guy's normal MEA meter and arranged to pay him at double the Bangkok city rate per kilowatt hour.

Meanwhile, with Moe and Sai at the pawnshop, the nasty neighbor guy came and carted off their refrigerator—stole it, really, right in front of the younger children. Told them that Mom and Dad owed him money, big time. They'd borrowed a bundle at two baht a day on a hundred baht per month. The high interest isn't a problem when you're dealing free and easy, but now, with Mom and Dad in jail, the cops had stopped all that.

The nasty neighbor guy wanted his money, so he grabbed what he could after the cops trashed the shack that second morning. He threw out the food in the fridge with the hungry children watching. Just for fun! He came back to look for more stuff later that same afternoon, but there wasn't anything else left to hock. Moe and Sai just stood there holding hands, crying silently.

Three days later, on Moe's ninth birthday, it all unraveled. The mean, nasty neighbor guy wouldn't stop, kept complaining about baby Gook keeping him awake all night with her crying. He made lots of racket about it to the community leader. She was horrified seeing the smelly, hungry kids with runny noses and baby with the runny bottom, plus the trashed house.

The community leader brought in her friend, the teacher from our slum kindergarten there. What to do with five children, abandoned, with a barely-nine-year-old and a seven-year-old trying to keep the family together?

They gathered some slum moms who all pitched in together. First they fed the older ones all they could eat (which was a lot) and gave the baby a bottle. Then they scrubbed down the kids, cleaned the house, washed the bedding and mosquito net, and gave baby Gook a well-used and well-loved teddy bear. They locked the shack door and moved all five to our kindergarten. The teacher stayed overnight, actually moved in to live in the school to give the children a home, till things were sorted out. That was eight years ago.

Now it's mostly better. Moe's grown up. On the way he was kicked out of the first grade for the "shoes incident." Said he'd never worn shoes in his whole life. Why did he have to wear shoes at school? He learned with his head and not his feet. That wasn't cool. First grader Master Moe walked.

That was just the first time he was kicked out of school. In the end he went through five schools—and he almost graduated from secondary school. Almost. Only two weeks to go and he had to run. He'd been too chummy with a girl classmate.

But now, months later, he has a real job. A teacher from that last reform school said, "I know that, deep down, this is a fine young man who needs a chance." He put in a good word for Moe, and we did too. He's seven months into being an apprentice welder/mechanic on a commercial ship plying the waters between Bangkok and Singapore. He went back to ask the girl he was chummy with to marry him.

She's graduated, has a job with the city of Bangkok. A proper girl. Moe asked our Sister Maria if Sister would "speak for him" to the girl's parents. He gave all the money he had for the dowry—five hundred baht. Moe is clean, has never touched drugs or alcohol.

His girlfriend grew up in the same slum. She lives with her parents. She wants Moe to show he can keep his job for one whole year first and made him promise her he would return to school to get his diploma.

Sai, his younger cousin, works in an open-air clothing market. She functions well in English. Makes good money. She rents a shack here in Klong Toey, where she's known and feels safe—and we pay her rent sometimes. She started rough. Left us at fifteen. Wanted to be on her own. Began making her living sassy-like, working as a "coyote girl" dancer. She smokes cigarettes, and her two little sisters berate her all the time. She's promised them she will quit. She hates drugs and still won't speak to her mother.

The next down the line is Master Dhuey. Finally, after six years of trying, a most zealous teacher taught him to read comic books and write his name. He left us last year at age fourteen. He's on the street at the moment but often returns home to his mom, who is out of prison now and works nights in Pattaya.

Now Dhuey's on the run. Thought he was cute, broke some slum rules. Payment was bruises and broken bones and left for dead. He wants to come back to live here at Mercy. Our men who work with street kids say we should let him stay on the street a while longer. He has to learn or die. We can't protect him.

And the two younger girls are doing well in school. Miss Gig acts tough, dresses like a thug, but always with pink bows in her hair or pink socks. She's cut a deal with our house mom to look the other way, most of the time, when Miss Gig wears lipstick. As long as she does her homework and house chores.

Her sister, baby Gook, still keeps her well-used, well-loved teddy bear from those days gone by. She loves to hear the old story about her crying and crying, keeping the mean, nasty neighbor awake all night.

And now and then, she rides city bus No. 205 from Klong Toey back home to her slum kindergarten to see the teacher who held her all those nights so she wouldn't be afraid after her momma was taken to prison. She says she will visit her momma sometime, but not now.

# Almost Sweet Sixteen

Gee and Kao don't look tough or mean. They just are. It's something you become when you grow up on the street. No tattoos, no long hair, not much swagger. Tattoos are for prison; swagger is for cool. These two young men of fifteen years are neither "prison" nor "cool." They're just pure essence of Bangkok street.

They met while foraging on the street. Though they never really "hung" together, they were street friends. That means loyalty. It also means they gave each other lots of space, never crowded each other, never pushed.

Gee is the first kid we ever met who was totally slapped around by 505, a newer combination of rubber cement and industrial paint thinner. It fits nicely in a pocket and can be discarded when a uniform shows up. Nobody ever notices it—except for the smell. Oh, it stinks! Not even garlic knocks out the smell.

Gee was living with his granny under a bridge near a brightly lit traffic intersection. When he got hungry enough or the 505 demanded his attention or Granny hollered at him loud enough, he would go clean automobile windshields for as long as it took to scrounge enough for food or 505.

Granny was weak and would walk around in slow motion, even on her spry days. Eventually we took Gee in and had one of our social workers look after Granny. Gee would still prepare her food every morning. He got up at dawn and bought rice and cooked it up before he went to our special Mercy Centre school for teenagers who never got any education when they were young.

Granny would always have her bad spells, but one day she was so decrepit, Gee got scared. Every day she was getting worse. Gee bought her food but she'd leave it untouched. Thankfully, she died in her sleep.

In preparing for the funeral and cremation, Gee couldn't memorize his prayers—for becoming a monk—"in front of the body" as we say, because the 505 had messed up his head. So on the day of Granny's cremation, the temple abbot, a kindly man, looked him over pretty well. Gee's eyes were clear; he was off the glue. So he allowed Gee to be a monk for a day to make merit for Granny. She'd always wanted that and had made him promise.

Kao came to us next. Kao's dad used to get him high on 505 and gave him broken beer bottles so he could cut himself on his arms, which made it more profitable when begging at traffic intersections. The drivers would see the blood and give money.

Kao's sister is in reform school. She never did drugs but had a mental breakdown after she saw "these two men on a motorcycle wearing helmets for disguise" shoot the only friend she ever had. That happened during the Klong Toey drug wars a couple of years ago.

The day her friend died, Kao's sister swallowed her whole stash of amphetamines—three pills, the equivalent of, say, a dozen big tablespoonfuls of coffee and sugar in one swallow. She was so jittery and crazy she went up on the third-floor roof and stood at the edge, having decided to fly off so she could go and see her dead friend in the storm clouds.

Kao tied a rope to himself and whispered to her gently that all would be OK. Like a skittish kitten, she believed him

**157**

long enough to watch him crawl out on the roof toward her. She didn't jump, but as she looked down she panicked and tottered. He grabbed her and the rope held. That is just one of Kao's defining moments of brotherly love.

These days both Kao and Gee are living in our Mercy Centre in one of our shelters for homeless kids, and that's where they met Miss Joop Jang, who lives in our home for children born with HIV. All three attend that special class, learning how to read and write.

Joop Jang is fifteen years old, our oldest surviving child born with HIV. As with most of our AIDS kids, her dad gave it to her innocent mom, who passed it along to innocent Joop Jang at birth. After Joop Jang's dad and mom died from the virus, she stayed with her granny. But then her granny got sick and couldn't care for her any longer, and that's when Joop Jang came to us.

Gee and Kao said Joop Jang reminded them of a girl they both knew on the street, another girl with AIDS who was killed by a hit-and-run truck. They watched her die right there on the street. Then they got hammered on 505 with her boyfriend to make her look of terrible pain and her final words—"Help me! Help me!"—go away. She died before they could get her to a hospital; they didn't have taxi money anyway.

But back to Joop Jang and her friendship with Kao and Gee ... Someone in their class started calling Joop Jang Miss Sweet Sixteen one day, and now they all do.

Their classroom is on the third floor of our office building across the street from the Mercy Centre. Since Joop Jang is often quite weak, her teacher asked Kao and Gee to carry her up the steps.

Miss Sweet Sixteen is painfully thin, almost weightless. She knows she isn't long for this world, but she won't let on. Although her teeth are crooked, what she does with them when she smiles lights up a room. Her life force is what won over Gee and Kao, I think. They know what fighting for survival is all about, and that gives them something in common.

Joop Jang continues on—three days well and four days sick, as we say in Thai. Sometimes she stays in bed all day by her oxygen tank. Occasionally she's hospitalized. But when she can make it to school, the boys treat her like Miss Sweet Sixteen, an age she probably will not live to see. She has a huge crush on them and they both are incredibly gentle with her. Oh, they love her! With a hard-core, street kid kind of love.

They are a happy threesome—Kao, Gee and Joop Jang. Someday the boys will grieve for their sister, Miss Sweet Sixteen, as will all of us, but through our tears, we will try to remember, "You should not grieve for those whose time has come."

# Living Past the Nightmare

This is one of those oh-yeah-I-kind-of-remember stories. Now that you mention it, whatever happened to those kids?

The *Bangkok Post* ran the original story in Perspective four years ago. There were six boys—the oldest fourteen, the youngest twelve and a few days—all sexually abused by foreign pedophiles. Heavy-duty-type abuse, for almost a whole year. The cops stumbled onto the story accidentally. There was an IT conference in London on criminal use of the Internet. Police from Thailand, attending the conference in the UK to update themselves, were shown some child porn downloaded from the Net. Folks there were saying, "Take a look at this stuff. Don't these boys look like they're Thai?"

The Thai officers smiled stiffly with their faces, not the tiniest twinkle in their eyes. Although no one noticed, they were saying quietly to each other through gritted teeth: "We'll be back home in Bangkok in two days."

And, oh, they didn't forget. They caught the gents in a heartbeat or two. The faces on the porn pictures from the Net were clear enough to identify a couple of the boys. The police asked if we knew the boys. It took some of our social workers who know the streets and the slums about an hour to track them down in Klong Toey, a neighborhood where everybody knows just about everybody else. The boys, by this time fed up with the abuse and broken promises, gladly led the cops to the bad guys and told them what they had done.

It wasn't pretty. This stuff never is. The gig went down like this.

The men were patient. A full week, they watched the boys at a well-known street corner where they sold flower leis and cleaned windshields with dirty rags. After they garnered a bit of cash, the boys usually went across the street to play computer games and a bit of snooker—just hang out like street kids looking for some action. That's where the men approached them.

First they gave them money. Then they invited them home with them and got them cleaned up. Deloused them and taught them how to take a "proper" bath. Later, in the police reports written by the boys, they told how the gents meticulously made sure the boys' bottoms were clean.

The boys were given new clothes and taken on trips to Pattaya. Usually overnight. The men gave them money for their families and encouraged them to go to school. The families winked to each other and took the money, mouthing how well their boys were doing in class. The families had pretty much forced the boys to drop out of school to work the streets. Booze had to be bought, gambling debts cared for.

Most evenings, the men gave the boys more money to play computer games—then took them back to their flats to play other games, taking photographs and making videos. Eventually, inevitably, the kids ran, and their families told them to go back. They enjoyed the money too. The families either didn't care or, more likely, didn't want to know. But the boys were spooked. Nice clothes no longer mattered. Money and cash even for mobile phones didn't count anymore. They ran back to the slums, but not to their parents. Instead they went to their grannies and lived with them.

We knew the boys. Knew their grannies too—some were in our Senior Citizens Group. We'd given rice, cooking oil and such to help them get by. These fine, stately, betel-nut-chewing ladies, sometimes with the granddads, their husbands, wouldn't have simply taken the rice and staples as a gift. No, they were "of an age" and "have face." So we'd stop by their homes—shacks—and say that the mom-and-pop neighborhood shop told us that Granny had paid for the rice but left it behind when she'd shopped. You know, the bag of rice was too heavy to carry ... That's the only way the grannies would have accepted it.

In Klong Toey, even more than in other places, dignity is most important. Often that's all the grannies have left. To take that from them is a blunder, an insensitivity beyond belief. And don't get me wrong. They also are quite choosy—especially selective about the betel they chew. There's betel nut and then there's betel nut. In Klong Toey dignity counts.

So too it was with the boys, who'd had their dignity stolen by the bad guys. It wasn't easy for the boys, being interviewed by the police and then again by the judge in the Juvenile Court. Being asked to look at the photographs the men had taken and put on the Internet. Writing a testimony, then telling the judge what happened. Then having the judge read it back to them word by word, seeking the truth. The interviews with the special police were videotaped too, and that brought back more bad memories. One of our social workers was there, and we tried to make it as comfortable as possible, but it wasn't nice, not at all.

The judge who handled the case was a good man and fair. The men went off to prison, and while the court case progressed, the boys were sent to a social welfare home some two hundred kilometers south of Bangkok, where they were cared for and sent to the remand school. Not that school was their first choice, but it was both for education and safety. Had they stayed in Bangkok, in Klong Toey, the families would have "gone belly-up," telling the boys to deny everything. No charges.

But staying in the remand school didn't last long. One by one the boys ran away from the home and returned to Bangkok. In a year all were home again, back with their grannies. But their time in the school was long enough for the court to process the case, to prosecute. The bad guys went to the slammer for a month of years. The boys were temporarily clean from the fatal 505 combo of thinner and glue, a viscous, yellowish goop that's sold in one of those brown energy drink bottles that are easy to discard when a cop shows up. They learned a bit of discipline and got a bit more reading, writing and arithmetic. Plus they actually admitted several times that they were happy and felt safe. But the lure of the streets is strong.

The boys are now older, more mature. The oldest are eighteen and mostly back on the streets. One of the older ones was just released from jail after ten months. His granny didn't visit because she didn't know which bus to take and was too ashamed to ask.

Another one they call Match Stick Head because of his unusual head shape. He has a younger brother and sister whom he cares for when he can. They don't know he runs just about anything that is non-taxable and black market that he can possibly carry on the back of his motorcycle. All they know is that he's gone a lot and generous when he's around. A real big brother, except he does act goofy. He tells them it's all the glue and thinner mix he sniffed when he was young. Even when you're off it for a while, the damage is done.

Three more are still on and off the glue and thinner mix, the 505. They're in and out of remand homes as well. Only one is going to school.

One boy you can find at a street corner, selling flower garlands that his granny makes. He gives her most of the money. Another one who is also there sometimes occasionally goes wacko and smears dirt and oil on a car windshield in a threatening matter. The police know him well, throw him into the slammer for two weeks to cool off. When they find the boys sniffing glue, they may just tell them to sit down outside the police station for a few days—don't go away, or else! You can't blame the police. What do you do? These boys won't stop until they want to … or until they're dead.

Another boy is a part-time motorcycle taxi driver. As I write this, he's back "inside." Racing his motorcycle and smelling of glue.

The 505 hasn't destroyed their brains entirely, by the way. You can talk to them about football. They still remember the names of all the players for Manchester United, and they know how Liverpool is doing. You look at them and they seem OK. Skinny and ragged around the edges, but OK. The glue-thinner combo doesn't leave any visible marks, but inside the scars run deep. It's like someone has stirred their brains with a stick. Or, as we say in Thai, their stability is like a twig stuck in some water buffalo poop alongside the road.

# The Revival of Cookie Crumb James

I t's funny what it takes sometimes to turn a life around. For Cookie Crumb James all it took was a tasty meal, some cookies ... and crumbs.

He came to us a total mess. Basket case material. Couldn't walk, couldn't crawl. Barely spoke (or didn't want to speak), large industrial-sized migraines that fried his brains. Not a friend in this world. He was born with HIV and has AIDS. Perfect example of a "throwaway kid." He was eight years old and large for an HIV/AIDS kid. That means normal size for a non-infected eight-year-old. Scarred face, bad left eye—shingles (herpes zoster) did that. But he ain't ugly! He's our Cookie Crumb James. You'd like him if you met him. Great lopsided grin.

When a child is brought to us out of nowhere—end of the line and "junked" on our doorstep—in hospice lingo we call that a "dump." A few days after the taxi dump at our Mercy Centre, we bestowed on Cookie Crumb James a special ribbon for bravery, valor and determination. But on the second day James slobbered rice gruel all over the ribbon. So much for valor.

We rarely do such ribbon ceremonies. In eleven years with AIDS children we've only bestowed a ribbon of honor once before—to a very special girl (but that's a story for another day).

Cookie Crumb James of the Soiled Ribbon decided to get better. Not right away. Nothing is ever that easy. The effort and energy you need to get well and just wanting to live can be an unbelievably difficult decision. But eventually, make the decision he did. Probably for lots of heavy-duty-type awesome reasons. But heck, on the surface, like so many of the "calls" that flip our lives upside down, Cookie Crumb James's biggest reason seemed so simple.

It came down like this. We took all the HIV/AIDS kids to a restaurant and carted Cookie Crumb James along. It was normal fare—add-water-stir-slowly-to-simmer-for-three-minutes kind of grub. But he went bonkers over the stuff. Claimed it was the best food he ever tasted. "Awesome!"

One of our very smart house moms cut a deal on the spot: "Kid, I'll change your Huggies quick when you stink and your bottom itches if you promise to walk. And when you walk, or even crawl, we'll all come here again, and you can have all you can eat."

The house mom figured that if she could get this kid up on his pins, walking, when he got that "morning urge," they could point him toward the toilet. One less stinky bottom! A smart lady.

The other kids picked up on this promise and began getting in Cookie Crumb James's face. Daring him to walk, calling him a sissy. Making him cry, making him angry. Besides, they didn't relish being downwind of Cookie Crumb James. He had a talent. Oh, he had a smelly talent! (The kids were also in favor of anything that would get them out on the town for an all-you-can-eat dinner.) But back to our first meeting with Cookie Crumb James ...

They brought him in a taxi from another hospice. Couldn't deal with his TB plus HIV/AIDS. Maybe they could have, maybe they couldn't—that wasn't our call. It was the end of the road for a double "throwaway" dead-end kid. And he smelled. Stank.

Even in those first moments with us, somehow we knew, as he sat propped up in a wheelchair, dripping poop, whimpering, that he was one of those special kids—"I dare you to take care of me and love me. Go ahead, just try, and I'll get better." Maybe all kids are that way. We probably were too.

They lugged him into an empty bed. A house mom slipped and grabbed his shirt. He almost hit his head, screamed, but she did catch him. That's all it took. Young James knew someone cared.

The first kid he met was Master Nok Yak (meaning "Giant Bird" in Thai), a scrawny, half-the-time sick seven-year-old who also has AIDS. He looks like a five-year-old, even after a full meal. Nok Yak walked over to the bed and held Cookie Crumb James by the hand. Offered him a bite of his cookie. Looking him over. Sizing him up. But something happened: they clicked. It was going to be OK. Cookies could be shared. Both of them throwaway kids, but who cares, as long as there is a supply of cookies? The rest would take care of itself.

For a year Cookie Crumb James wasn't fun. Didn't like himself very much. Didn't like what the virus was doing to him. Spent a lot of time in bed with raging headaches. They massaged his forehead for ten to fifteen minutes a couple of times a day. Then put an ice-cold cloth on his forehead. He would stop whimpering till the cloth warmed or he fell asleep. The house mom was mostly rough and often impatient with him, but after you've been abandoned, just wearing clean diapers, getting massaged, having an ice-cold cloth on your forehead—these little things seem like heaven.

And his friendship with Giant Bird bloomed. At mealtime this scrawny seven-year-old kid would wander over to Cookie Crumb James's bed and help feed him. The first spoonful went in the mouth, the second spoonful slipped accidentally—ho! ho! ho!—smearing food in his face and hair. Usually Cookie Crumb James cried. Sometimes, when the headache wasn't too bad, he and Giant Bird would giggle and laugh. But James was eating regularly, gaining strength. One day, when the food smearing wasn't fun, he kicked Nok Yak with his good leg. Nok Yak cried and kicked back. Cookie Crumb James cried too. Trouble. And then more trouble: the house mom cuffed them both and gave them some sharp words. She had had a fight with her drunk husband the night before, and a few other kids in her care were really sick.

So young James got stubborn. Said he could feed himself. It started off with his mouth in the plate, like a puppy dog. But the other kids made fun of him, so he got his good arm in action and started to hold a spoon. Kind of.

And his house mom, for months she scolded and scolded. Told him to walk. Called him a sissy. But she knew the rules. Knew how much Cookie Crumb James could handle. She had that gift. When Nok Yak, alias Giant Bird, teased mean or played too hard, she chased him away. She's a beat-up slum lady with an end-of-the-line job. Caring for dead-end, throwaway kids and cleaning toilets. But she loves kids, can't help herself.

Forced into the unwanted job of being a surplus mom, she didn't want to get too close to the kids like a real mom. She has her own kids—tattoos and trouble, but they are alive and not sick. She doesn't know if she can handle the eventual visit to the temple. Cookie Crumb James and his pals with AIDS like Giant Bird always make that last journey. To go, not to return. To sleep, not to wake. Death with no escape.

Cookie Crumb James has been with us seventeen months now, and at nine years of age is starting first kindergarten, just a year behind his friend Giant Bird. James can't see well out of his left eye, but his right eye is almost fine. The daytime Huggies are gone. He can talk clearly (when he tries) and understands everything. The house mom loads up his lunch with two or three cookies, and he shares them with everyone but cries when there's none left for him.

Several weeks back he and Bird trashed his makeshift wheelchair. A bright red toy cart with a round steering wheel—no pedals, just rubber wheels. He propelled it by pushing forward on the floor with his good leg. Oh, did he and Giant Bird ever total out that poor wheelchair cart! It happened like this. The daily time trials were on. Cookie Crumb James propped up, riding that toy cart like he was a wild Formula One driver with Giant Bird pushing him from behind. They'd crash into everything—walls, pillars, potted plants, other kids. They'd crash and bruise and laugh and sometimes cry. Part of getting well and just being boys.

And then one day they got up from a crash. Its bent wheels stuck, the cart wouldn't move. So James took his first steps and Big Bird held onto him until they both fell down. They giggled and laughed on the floor. Stayed down there a good while, resting, because kids with AIDS can play hard but they don't have a lot of energy, and it takes them a long time to catch their breath.

But get up they finally did, and Cookie Crumb James took another step. Then one day he stumbled down the stairs. Oh dear, the house mother told him good riddance, to come back up himself or he'd get no supper. Took him two hours, and she wouldn't let anyone help him. But a kindly volunteer who happens to be a physiotherapist did encourage him, that day and every day. Now James walks about a hundred meters to school every day and falls down only a couple of times. Not too shabby for a throwaway kid. Guess that other hospice didn't know he was Cookie Crumb James of the Soiled Ribbon.

We know little about his past. His parents were itinerant construction workers. Mom is AIDS dead, but he has a dad and a grandma somewhere. Also there's a healthy sister a year older. We're trying to find her, don't think she knows.

Meanwhile Cookie Crumb James is thriving. Broken walking, loopy left arm and a lopsided grin. Giant Bird is still his best friend, and they fight a lot, make up, play and fight again. That house mom doesn't call him a sissy anymore. Yes, that last trip to the temple—one day at a time. And Cookie Crumb James knows he has a real mom.

I said just above that he and Giant Bird play and fight a lot. That's not totally true now. Presently half-the-time sick, Giant Bird is only making it to kindergarten about one or two days a week. Now it's Cookie Crumb James who comes and holds Giant Bird's hand and helps feed him. First spoonful in his mouth, second spoonful all over his face and hair.

On his strong days Cookie Crumb James walks, dragging his bum leg along slowly so Giant Bird can keep up. Their classmates don't poke fun anymore. And everyone is gentle to Giant Bird. Yes, kids can be cruel, but mostly they are kind. They know no self-pity. That has to be taught.

This is one of those "great stories." Saying that there is good in this world and dreams that are worth fighting for, that we should never give up. Really. Saying that down deep all of us are dead-end throwaway kids. Cookie Crumb James and Giant Bird are the stronger ones.

Last Saturday morning, after antivirals and breakfast, the house mom baked some cookies with the children. Out in our yard is a small cement pond with water lilies. Someone making merit bought half a dozen fish, freeing them into the pond. Cookie Crumb James had located a fishing hook with some string. He and Bird stuffed their pockets with fresh baked cookies and, grinning, walked over to the pond, hoping that maybe the fish like cookies.

He came to us a child without time and without space. Cookie Crumb James.

# Every Picture Tells a Story

We've got the one family picture of Puk Pik, and that's it—a picture that his dad somehow missed when trashing the rest. Taken eight years ago when he was a baby, maybe six months old, with his real mom holding him and his dad standing by. Puk Pik is nine now, an orphan until a few weeks ago. A slum-dressed lady who said she was his auntie brought him to us and then disappeared into the dawning day.

Now there's proof of his past. We found Dad—hiding, avoiding us, whatever you want to call it—and Dad had the picture. Puk Pik's dad had kept the picture hidden almost nine years from his new wife. He knew she'd go into a rage because he promised she was the only one. His first and only. He told our social workers his new wife doesn't know about his HIV either.

Puk Pik's dad does take his antiviral medicine regularly. About a year ago, totally out of the blue, he came to the Mercy Centre , asking us to help him get the medicine. He had no idea his son was here, probably no idea he was even alive. Only later, comparing notes at a staff meeting, did we realize, "Hey, this cat is Puk Pik's dad."

Last month a fabulous Thai football school accepted Master Puk with a full scholarship. This is a really big deal. He passed his academic exams and they had him show his stuff on the pitch. They interviewed him for over an hour. He passed everything, but there was a condition. To save a place for him, they urgently needed some basic documentation. Birthplace, parents' names, etc. Otherwise no football scholarship, which could change his whole life.

We found Dad after the good folks at the National Registration Bureau did a computer search. We knew Puk Pik's family name. Auntie had told us that when she had brought him in a few months after the baby picture was taken.

Auntie had come early on a rainy morning, just at the time when the dogs stop their nighttime barking in Klong Toey. In a hurry, in tears, totally distraught, with the taxi waiting, she said "they" were after her and wanted to hurt her. She was afraid they would kidnap Puk Pik. Would we care for him till she could come back ... someday?

More than eight years ago, armed with his family name at the Registration Bureau, we came up with a list of possible relatives. It still took over a week. First to the municipal district office, then the police station, then the local postman. We were knocking on doors, and folks were suspicious. "Why do you want to know?"

When Auntie answered the door, she was cautious but friendly. She said the danger facing her when she'd brought the boy to our door had long passed, but she's still constantly on the run, now selling trinkets on footpaths to tourists. Each time the uniforms take her to the station, they fine her four hundred baht and sometimes take her stuff. But she was totally relieved to learn her nephew was alive. She thought that he'd died of AIDS and that we'd come to take her to the temple for his cremation. We showed her his latest picture in his football uniform, and she kissed it and kissed it, so grateful that her nephew had escaped the deadly virus and was healthy.

Good old Dad was not so helpful, but he was there also, at the family house that was registered in Auntie's name. Dad, who'd always had a mean streak, had married again. He wouldn't talk, denied everything—that he had been married before, that he'd ever had a son, that he had HIV. He denied the whole ball of wax.

So we left him and came back with a couple of lads we know to have a "friendly conversation" with good old Dad. Shortly into the conversation he began talking politely. He even found the picture, said he'd forgotten to throw it out with the rest he got rid of so his new wife wouldn't find out. He's ailing now and doesn't get out of the house much.

Then Auntie told us about the horrible tragedy that had taken Puk Pik's mom, her little sister. No matter how you try to dress it up and explain it away, suicide is suicide.

Puk Pik's parents had been living with Auntie in the house when Dad walked. There'd been a huge fight. He blamed Puk Pik's mom for giving him AIDS, which was not true. Dad slapped Mom, knocked her down, kicked her and slapped their six-month-old baby. She grabbed a kitchen knife, but he got out the door before she got to him. He never came back, not while she was alive anyway.

Dad was a gambler. The fight had started when he told Mom to start working nights in a bar—hustle drinks, do whatever it took to make gambling money for him. She said no. She wouldn't sell drugs and she wouldn't run an illegal "ping-pong" lottery out of their house. Good old Dad ran from the knife, and she chased him down the street until she couldn't run any more. A neighbor calmed her down.

Mom was from a good family. The relatives had told her to stay away from "that man," but she hadn't listened. First love is sure that nothing can go wrong.

Now she had the virus, but she was still healthy. Mom stayed in the house with baby Puk Pik, but her husband's associates kept coming around. They weren't nice people—they wanted payment for her husband's gambling debts. She was breast-feeding Puk Pik at the time. The medical people said that wasn't good, but there was no money to buy powdered milk. We found out later that Puk Pik didn't get the virus. Luck of the draw.

Mom couldn't pay the debts and there was nowhere to run. As Auntie tells it, her little sister told her what she was going to do. Said big sis couldn't stop her because she was convinced it was for the best. She knelt down and begged forgiveness from her baby, and she begged her sister to pray for her—to make merit—for the proper three days at the temple, and to bring her son with her. Her sister honored these last requests—almost. She and the neighbors got together enough money for two nights of chanting. The monks did double duty the second night as is common to complete all the necessary chants and prayers.

Baby Puk Pik was at the temple in his aunt's arms. At six months old he was too young to be ordained as a monk and make merit as a loyal son for his mom. So Auntie convinced a neighbor's boy to become a monk for the two-day ceremony and pray for her dead sister.

Auntie did not have money to give the neighbors to care for the baby while she was selling her trinkets, so she carried him with her, constantly in fear of the uniforms. When her trinkets didn't sell well, she did a bit of begging with baby Puk Pik at her feet, asleep beside her. But she swears she never gave him drugs to make him sleep.

The penalty for begging with a baby the first time you're caught is thirty days, plus they take the baby away. One evening another beggar spotted the uniforms coming and told her to run with the baby. She hid till early morning. Then a taxi driver she knew from school drove her to the Mercy Centre.

175

She came to visit a couple of times, always looking over her shoulder. She told us his full name, but she didn't have any documents. She saw that he was well cared for. Then she disappeared.

Puk Pik is one of those kids who are like the sunshine. He wakes up at dawn and says, "Today is going to be the best day of my life."

Our Sister Maria told him he has powerful angels. The angels must have joined with Saint Anthony (the patron saint of locating lost articles) to find us proof to take to the football school. One picture, so that this fabulous kid can have a chance for a good education and take advantage of his talents, and know what his mom and dad looked like. We keep the original in the safe and Puk Pik has a good copy. He's taped it to his locker door at football school.

He's been at the school almost a month now. Says he's over being homesick. He has lots of friends and practices football every afternoon after class. The school sent a report that he's fitting in well, both in the classroom and on the football pitch. He's happy, not yet a star, but he's working at it.

Not long ago Dad got back to us and asked for the boy's address at the school so he could write to him. We're leaving it up to Puk Pik. He's almost ten years old now and has a mind of his own.

# Miss Pim Gets Second and Third Chances

**M**iss Pim had been with us for nine years. She was sixteen, third in her high school class, gentle as gentle can be, with a smile to warm the hardest of hearts. One Sunday morning about a year ago, she handed me a wrinkled piece of paper, a note she had written in her own hand.

Pim's note and her story are important because she is a "throwaway" orphan kid who made it. Lots of kids, but especially these so-called throwaways, need to be walked through the bad patches, not just once but many times before they reach adulthood.

On that Sunday when she handed me the note, I knew the contents were grave. Pim had that limp, wilted, beaten-up look of a teenager in mourning at a temple cremation, standing in front of the furnace when the temple manager zips open the red plastic body bag in the coffin to offer one last glance at a dead friend as the monks are chanting their final chant. Grieving for someone who has died before their time. Utter despair. Absolute misery. It was that kind of look she gave me. If you've seen it once, you never forget it.

The note she handed me was torn from a school notebook—a last will and testament, really. It said that she was leaving us to work as a bar hostess in Pattaya. There was a pimp from the slum who could get her into a bar. Said she wouldn't have to pay him much, that she'd make good money the first few weeks because she was "new." Said he'd look after her, discreetly, so the authorities would look the other way. True, the authorities would check her out, but not too closely. Business is business.

As I read, panic and shock set in, as if she not only had been kidnapped for ransom but had kidnapped herself for her own ransom. And her graciousness only made it worse. I knew she could just walk away, down a path from which she would never return.

Goodness gracious! It turned out her mom was AIDS sick, dying in a charity ward of a Bangkok government hospital. Mom owed a few big notes from a handful of unlucky card games a while back. When the thugs she owed the money to heard that she was sick, they sent a collector to visit her in the hospital. Not a pleasant scene, but debts are debts and business is business. Nothing personal, you understand.

To compound the mother's money problems, her doctor had prescribed some last-ditch expensive medicines that were not on the government list. Mom didn't have the necessary cash. The doctor told her these meds would not save her life, just make her passing a bit easier.

Mom was terrified of death. For years she had been a nighttime "fortune-teller/masseuse" by trade outside and inside a "one star" hotel. But this time she couldn't pretend to know the future, and she was afraid—especially afraid that without her daughter Pim no one would take her body to the temple for prayers.

Sick Mom had told the collector to go see her daughter. Maybe Pim could do a few chores after school in the afternoons. The collector confronted Pim on her way back from school and told her the money was needed to save her mom's life. And now, on that Sunday, Pim was saying she was leaving us to hustle some money for good ol' Mom.

This is how the collection game is played. The hired gun gets a hundred baht for every thousand baht collected. The real boss, in the shadows, usually throws in a can of Chemical Mace for the hired gun to carry, just in case the debtor is impolite. Pim's mom was no stranger to Mace cans.

Pim is petite. Didn't eat well in her early years. She was the youngest of three children and was born, literally, on a small wooden footbridge not far from her house in Ayutthaya. Mom was pregnant with Pim when she ran away from her husband, and she gave birth just before she found shelter. Babies choose their own time.

A few days later Mom left her other children, a son and daughter, with her husband's parents, who were poor rice farmers, and she brought her new baby to Klong Toey. Here she hooked up with a one-legged guy who made his living begging on the streets. She married him for survival, not love. He made enough money as a beggar for the family to get by. Trouble was, he drank most of the money. Pim's mom had to find her own work, so she called herself a fortune-teller/ masseuse and made up attractive lies for passersby inside and outside one of the city's larger cheap hotels.

When the booze flowed at home, Pim's mom and one-legged stepdad fought hard, and somehow during these fights Pim got beaten up too. This went on for years, until Pim was just old enough for kindergarten and her mom dumped the one-legged guy and took off with a quack medicine guy. This new guy drove around in a claptrap pickup truck and loudspeaker from village to village, selling cure-all potions.

The quack medicine guy wasn't into kids, so before running off, Mom sweet-talked a neighborhood lady into watching out for Pim for a few days. Mom would pay the freight when she returned. The neighbor didn't love the child or show any affection. One reason was, a few days became a year and Pim's real mom conveniently forgot to send money for food, board and clothing. But at least this neighbor lady didn't beat Pim, plus she did feed her, and during this period in her life, Pim went to school.

Pim finished kindergarten and was in the middle of first grade when her real mom returned and went back to the one-legged man. The booze and fighting resumed, and Pim was caught in the crossfire once again. She dropped out of school.

When Pim was seven, a local policeman brought her to our Mercy Centre. She was pretty much black and blue, skinny and hungry, but safe with us. After she recovered from her latest bruising, we put her in one of the neighborhood schools.

Years passed, and Pim's grades were good. She continued to live in our shelter for older girls and showed a knack for English. Slowly she made her own way, gaining confidence, and gentle Pim became a leader and role model among our girls. We prayed there would be no more bumps in her road.

Pim had escaped from a world of trouble, but her older sister Noi wasn't nearly as lucky. Noi had been living all this time with her elderly grandparents in Ayutthaya, until they could no longer care for her properly. A neighbor who was a drunk had been abusing Noi, a pretty girl but a slow learner, and the police would not intervene—the abuser had powerful drinking friends.

The grandparents had no recourse, no one to turn to. Plus they didn't know their daughter's situation in the city. So they sent Noi to her mom, who was now sick with AIDS and still living with the one-legged guy. He started using

Noi until eventually Noi, too, showed up on our doorstep, heavily pregnant and beaten black and blue.

This was the same week the collector came to see Pim and told her to give him cash. On the day Pim gave me the note, we told her she was a true heroine, among the most loyal of daughters to walk the earth, but if she had even one brain cell in her skull she had to stay in school.

That same afternoon we walked five minutes with Pim down the slum railroad tracks to a popular four-table noodle shop. The collector's mom owned the shop. Seems she and Pim's mom, though never close friends, knew each other years ago when they were both young and pretty. And we knew the collector himself from many years back when as a child he had learned to read and write in one of our slum kindergartens.

We ate our noodles. Came time to pay, we secretly had given Pim the money for the noodles plus an extra thousand-baht note. She paid the bill and laid down the extra note— slum-style. There are rules and customs to be followed in Klong Toey. Walking out, we whispered, "Leave the girl alone! Enough is enough."

Decorum and dignity had been served. No collector would bother her again. Pim was safe. Then we got her mom out of the hospital and brought her to our AIDS hospice, where she died of virulent TB a few days later.

At the temple the monks chanted the customary three days of prayers in one sitting so we could cremate the body on the same day. There was only one small wreath. The collector brought it. Always best in his business to keep good relations, especially with the deceased. As it turned out, he and his noodle shop mom were the only ones at the temple besides us.

Two months later the one-legged guy died of AIDS. That's about the same time we discovered that he had given the virus to Pim's sister Noi, who gave birth shortly afterwards—before going over the edge. She walked away one morning. We've looked everywhere. Now we fear the worst. Noi's story is too painful to tell right now, and this is Pim's story. But I do wish to mention that to everyone's delight and surprise, Noi's baby, a beautiful girl nicknamed Miss Grasshopper, is healthy. Luck of the draw. Tested negative, does not have the virus. She remains in our care as a gift of great joy and hope in our house.

Meanwhile Pim has stayed in school, continuing to excel, everybody's favorite teenager. She was recently awarded a two-year scholarship in a wonderful international baccalaureate program. Wow! But the path is never smooth, is it? She needed a passport.

Her mom was dead, and Mom's stories to Pim had been that her dad was dead too. You know … he was drunk and plowed full-speed-ahead into a pillar on a stolen motorcycle, or had been bitten by a deadly snake or shot dead for being in the wrong place at the wrong time—whatever! This meant that Pim was legally an orphan and an official ward of the Thai courts. It also meant that she would need a signature from a children's court judge to qualify for a passport.

During the application process, as we unraveled the red tape in a government office in Bangkok where there is a computer that keeps track of such things, we learned that her dad was in fact alive and living with his parents in Ayutthaya. We figured getting his signature on a form would be easier than going to court, so Pim, along with staff, went to find her dad.

He had moved. It took a series of false leads and wrong roads and seven-hour drives upcountry to find him. But he really was alive. He's a fifty-seven-year-old cow herder. A hired hand watching some forty head of Brahman cattle. He's got a weather-beaten face and is a bit deaf. A simple man who doesn't talk a lot. He accompanied us back to Bangkok to scratch an "X" and leave a thumb print on the forms and swear an oath of paternity.

On the way to Bangkok in the van, Pim suddenly realized that she had gone from being an orphan to having a dad. She was so shaken, sitting next to him for the first time, that she remained silent the entire ride.

We took Pim and her dad to the government offices, jumped through all the official hoops and then sent him back home again. And that, we thought, was that. But it turned out that, before we could satisfy all the bureaucrats, Pim's father had to make two more trips to Bangkok.

Finally, all the i's were dotted and all the t's crossed. Sending her dad back home for the final time, at the bus station Pim asked him, "Why didn't you ever come find me?" First he shrugged, and then he cried.

These days Pim is taking a crash course to improve her English in preparation for her studies abroad. Not a doubt in the world that she will graduate, and wouldn't it be fabulous if she gets a university scholarship? The first in her family to get beyond the fourth grade. Says someday she wants kids of her own, to give them—and every kid she meets—all the love she never got.

She also mentioned that she would like to visit her grandparents again, and to take along her niece, Miss Grasshopper. Her grandparents are both over ninety and not in the best of health. Pim would like to seek their blessing.

# It's All in the Game

It's a love story that needs telling. Three of the most fabulous children on the planet and their giggles galore version of *pong pae* —something like blind man's buff, with a Thai whiff of hide and seek added for spice.

It's a glorious game. *Pong pae* means something like "Thumbs up—I found you!" And you say the word *pong* loudly as you hold up your thumbs when you find the person who is hiding.

Except our Miss Phae can't quite manage the word *pong*, so the other two cut her a bit of slack, letting her just say *dhaah*. Plus she isn't sure about her thumbs, so she gets to raise up her whole arm. Actually Miss Phae is probably the best player. Yes, she's blind, but she can really hear! That's her secret weapon.

And *pae* is what you say when you touch whoever is "it"—the one who is looking for you—but you find them first and touch them before they see you. That's when you say *"Pae!"*

Now Miss Rin, way oldest of the three, considers herself most certainly the best *pong pae* player in all of Thailand, maybe even the planet. It's a matter of "face." Besides that, she's the "older sister" and almost their real momma.

But here's what happened last week. She goofed up big time. These are fragile kids, and when big sister Rin told them she wouldn't be around to play anymore, couldn't play anymore, because she planned to run away, it pretty much destroyed them. Miss Phae just held on to Miss Phon and wouldn't let her go. For hours. And Miss Phon, well, she wouldn't let anyone change her Huggies, and that soon became quite noticeable. And most scary of all, they wouldn't take their antivirals. These kids know—oh yes, they know—that to miss your a.m./p.m. antivirals just a few times is fatal. Truly fatal.

Miss Rin is kind of complicated. In the middle of last week, one of the other girls in the house laughed when Miss Rin said something. Miss Rin is really sensitive. She knows all the words, but with her deformed palate, sometimes the sounds get mixed up. When the other girl laughed, Miss Rin lost it. Tears, hysteria. She ran immediately to a house mom whom she loves and trusts. The house mom had seen this before, so she held Miss Rin tightly for a long time. Miss Rin gets the shakes, which in a heartbeat can quickly turn into shock, with the whites of her eyes rolling up, if the trusted house mom doesn't hold her and comfort her and calm her down.

So Friday, two days later, Miss Rin decided. She made sure her two little sisters had eaten but didn't tell them she was leaving. After dark Miss Rin put on her "going outside the building shoes"—slip-ons because she never mastered shoelaces. Climbed down the drain pipe, over the gate. Off to find Mr. Dhoot—her "kinda" boyfriend. She said once that he used to hold her, make her feel good. Seems they were on the streets together a couple of years back. She hasn't seen him since. We don't know much. Don't know what he looks like, don't know if he even exists. But for sure, somebody sweet-talked her back then.

Miss Rin remembers his name and that he's not old and they were *giks* (casual romantic partners or sexual liaisons).

**185**

That's how she contracted the virus, or so we guess. She decided to go back and live under the bridge where she used to, where the limping dog was, the one she saw the car hit. But the last time she'd gone back, she said "they" had moved the bridge because she couldn't find it. But maybe she could find it this time.

The dog didn't have a name, so she simply had called it Dog. Miss Rin didn't have a name either, just Rin. But that's enough, isn't it? We've asked her who gave her the name Rin, but she goes glassy eyed when we do, so we don't go there anymore. Simply says her name is Rin. Says it was at that bridge where she'd met her *gik*, Mr. Dhoot. She felt if she could find him, he would hold her and make her feel good again, and he would save her from girls laughing at the way she talked. But really, all he had done for her before was to give her AIDS. That doesn't make him one of our favorite people.

A fast-thinking house mom, the one who held her, saw Miss Rin climb over the gate. A wise woman, she decided to let Miss Rin go her merry way but quietly follow her. And so she did. Miss Rin wandered till almost dawn, stopping to forage a couple of garbage bins for food. Then at pre-dawn she found a dark corner under a footbridge and lay down to sleep. A drunk guy came by, but not that drunk, and saw her asleep. Definitely not a cool situation. A slum dog had come and snarled, but not enough to scare him away. The house mom had already phoned a neighborhood policeman, and he came on his motorcycle. The drunk moved on.

Miss Rin was awake and crying. Our house mom came up to her, asked if she wanted to come home and Rin said no. Oh boy! Then the wise house mom told a small fib, said Miss Rin's two little sisters had been crying all night long. Then she told the big truth—that without their big sister, their "Almost Momma" Rin, they couldn't play *pong pae* . That did it. She came home.

Dawn was just breaking, and her little sisters were waking up, so Miss Rin, Almost Momma, was home in time to help them bathe and brush their teeth. Also, on the way back, Miss Rin wanted the slum dog to come. Our wise house mom agreed, if the dog wanted to stay.

So then we had a new dog. Even with regular food, though, he didn't stay long. But Miss Rin had come home to stay. She and the girl who had laughed at her made up and now are the best of friends.

Miss Rin is up early to be Almost Momma each morning for the other girls and to send Miss Phon off to special school. Miss Phon is ninety percent blind but loves school and can sing songs and answer at roll call when the teacher calls out her name. When anyone asks her what her favorite game is, she says loudly *"Pong pae !"* Her friend Miss Phae also does quite well, moving around with her walker. While Miss Phon is in school, she and Miss Rin listen to music on the radio. Miss Rin in her free time finds pictures in movie magazines and says that the boys there almost look like her *gik*, Mr. Dhoot.

One more thing. As we said, Miss Phon can't see very well. They were playing their last late afternoon *pong pae* game before supper. They had a huge to-do as Miss Phon walked into a wall and had a big bump on her forehead and cried and cried that Miss Rin didn't tell her about the wall. And Miss Rin could only hold her, hug her, until Miss Phon suddenly stopped crying, realizing she was hungry. It's Miss Rin's chore to make sure the girls eat regularly because they have to take the antivirals according to when they eat.

Tomorrow is another day, with plenty of time for another game of *pong pae* .

# PART IV

Holy Days

# A Christmas Lullaby (2004)

The cook found them at the side entrance just before dawn, when you could still make out the stars: six-year-old Fon, her mom and our ferocious, slum-born, streetwise guard dog, all curled up asleep together. The "ferocious" guard dog, by the way, in spite of all training to the contrary, welcomes strangers. The more shabbily they dress, the more friendly he becomes.

Fon became our Christmas present, coming to stay with us for a while to share her wisdom and joy—her dance, her song, her innocence. And she led us as we followed the Magi and the Christmas star.

She's a special little girl who at the age of six is still learning to walk and talk, but she knows how to dance and sing. Something went terribly wrong when she was born. Baby Fon didn't get enough oxygen. So later in a rented room, with Dad sick and Mom working, she had no real social contact. She walks at her own pace and mostly without help, and her dancing is graceful but slow as she's careful not to stumble and fall. She's still not too good at talking, but she can sing quietly, crooning without words.

She usually tags around with Dao—glorious Miss Dao—who, at three-and-a-half years of age, decided to become Fon's "older" sister. It was Dao who took Fon's hand and led her everywhere. And it was Dao who taught her how to sing.

Our sacred stories and legends tell of wise men, astrologers—scientific intellectuals, really, who'd probably read the Hebrew scriptures—who with prophetic wisdom followed the star shining in the East which led them to Bethlehem.

Angels were in the high heavens singing, telling the shepherd families, who probably had also seen and been mystified by the star, about a special child born on this day. They were told to go to Bethlehem town, over the hills, not far, where they found the child lying in a manger near an inn.

I think about Joseph and Mary standing in line, travel weary, stamping their feet and trying to keep warm. Winter can be cold in that part of the world. Forced to report for a government census, they had traveled on foot and by donkey some eighty kilometers from Nazareth. Tradition suggests that the journey took them nine days. The innkeeper, perhaps a compassionate man, looked at this pair, dressed like vagabonds, who sounded like people from the north—Galilee—and told them he was truly sorry, but the inn was full. There was no room.

Then a kindly voice—perhaps the innkeeper himself, maybe his wife, perhaps an angel who'd noticed their plight and Mary's heavily pregnant state—mentioned a place nearby where animals were stabled. Desperate to get out of the cold, they made it to the stable.

And maybe it was also that way with Fon and her mom. Perhaps a kindly voice had said, "There's a place in the Klong Toey slums where maybe you can go. A woman and her small daughter would be safe there."

That morning Fon's mother begged our cook to look after her precious only daughter, just for a while, so that she could take care of a pressing matter. She said she'd be back and, tears in her eyes, disappeared into the early dawn. It was that "ferocious" guard dog of ours, who kept licking Fon's face, plus several cookies from the cook—one for the dog, one for Fon, then two for Fon, so she could give one to the dog—that persuaded the girl to come inside.

A couple of days later we discovered that Fon couldn't hear. A bit of warm olive oil soon solved that problem. We made sure that the first thing she heard was the pealing of a tiny silver bell, like angels singing in the heavens. That beautiful sound elicited her first smile.

The second big smile came with the ice cream cone. She was afraid of it at first. An ice cream cone is cold to the touch and can look scary if you've never seen one before. So Dao, who knows lots about ice cream, licked her own cone first, showing Fon that it was OK, and that second smile came with her first tentative taste of the confection. Wow!

Dao showed her our Christmas crib, and immediately Fon lay down and went to sleep. The dog came and curled up beside her. She slept with a smile on her face. The dog snored. They dreamed together.

Two thousand years before, Joseph also had a dream— to take the child and Mary and run away. Run now, in the middle of the night! They're coming to kill your child. Maybe both of you too.

We learned later, when she came back, that Fon's mom had also been forced to run. No, they weren't coming to kill her or her child, but it was something almost as horrible. Some Slimy Slipperies were forcing Fon's mom to do some bad stuff that you don't even want to think about, to pay back some loans—three times over. Cash she'd borrowed for her husband when he was dying of that unpopular disease. She didn't give up, and by a stroke of good luck, or maybe through the intercession of an angel, she found a policeman, a good man, boyhood best chum of her husband's, to come to their defense. People said that there'd been loud shouting, the sound of gunshots. The Slimy Slipperies had slunk off—back into the darkness.

She was still poor when he died, but at least she was safe. Unharmed. Debts canceled. So poor that the friendly Buddhist abbot lifted the lid of the box holding donations for the destitute and allowed her to take enough so that merit could be made and the monks could chant the holy sutras.

It's Christmas. The Holy Season. Let us look for the star. Let us try to understand and not be afraid of the heavens and cosmic events. Let us take that journey to Bethlehem. And if, on our journey, we should meet Fon and her mom sleeping on the pavement, before dawn, when we can still see the stars—sleeping all curled up with a doubly ferocious, slum-born, streetwise guard dog who welcomes strangers—let's stop and invite them in. Maybe even offer them some cookies.

# Miss Peh and the Piano Man:
## An Easter Letter

Everyone who meets her even once says "Wow!" What a special child! She's precious and precocious. But with lots of catching up to do. Lots and lots. She's gone through many a bad patch.

She caught HIV from her innocent mom at birth, who got it from her not very innocent dad, and now her eyes don't work well at all. They did for a while over a year ago, when she first came here. But after that the virus turned nasty and beat up her optic nerves. Lately her eyes don't work well even on bright sunshiny days. She's blind.

And beautiful she is. A gift. We're absolutely convinced that she is some former grand noble lady, born outside her proper time and place, whom you might read about in ancient books of lore. This fragile, precocious, "just catching up" seven-year-old little girl with the virus has still got her baby teeth. She smiles when you ask her to and sits up now by herself and can manage her arms and hands into a beautiful *wai* of greeting. Not yet totally cool on feeding herself, but we're working on that, along with her walking.

Life did not start well for Miss Peh. Her dad met the virus in some unmade bed on a booze-filled night. Mom never knew till almost two years later, when she was pregnant with baby Peh and a routine hospital pregnancy blood test showed she was HIV-positive. Dad died first, Mom later, just a few weeks after she gave birth to her first and only daughter. That was seven years ago.

Granny cared for baby Peh as long as she could, living in a rented shack room about the size of a mosquito net. Then baby Peh moved in with her auntie, a street sweeper with three children and a motorcycle taxi driver husband. Peh was almost five and couldn't, or wouldn't, walk or talk. By that time Auntie knew about the virus, and her auntie did not dare tell her husband.

During the day there was no one to care for Peh, with Auntie sweeping the streets, Uncle working long hours as a motorcycle taxi driver and their three children in school. Do what you can! They put her on the floor next to some freshly cooked rice, locked the door and came back in the evening.

Auntie was afraid her husband would find out about the virus, get angry and leave her and her three children. Plus she didn't like keeping secrets from him. She'd never done that. A neighbor told her about a day care center—an 8:00 to 5:00 p.m. affair. The staff asked the big question. Auntie said yes. They frowned, hemmed and hawed, and politely gave Auntie our phone number. That's how Miss Peh came to us.

Auntie visited once. That was a year ago. She promised to come often. How does that expression go? "Don't hold your breath!"

Miss Peh cries when the older children touch her unexpectedly. Surprising her. Frightening her. When they don't talk to her first so she can recognize their voices, their smell. She's as timid as a fawn.

And then there was this piano guy, fiancé of a nice lady who comes to visit. He stopped by to play a song or two. The kids listened politely to bits of the Hallelujah Chorus of Handel's *Messiah*, but five-year-olds, even six- and seven-year-olds, tire easily with unfamiliar classics. Miss Peh was in the back. Sitting in the lap of Momma Gung. Crippled beat-up Momma Gung, off the streets, who wandered into Klong Toey and then walked, hobbled really, to our doorstep. Said she had no one, nowhere to go. We said, you can stay three days to catch your breath—a clean bed and some food. That was four years ago. Now she loves Miss Peh for all the children she will never have.

When the piano guy came, Miss Peh had had a bad morning. Some of the children had teased her. And tears and whimpers are her only defense. We thought the music might soothe her. We believe in the magic of music. The children know how to sing scales. So we asked the piano guy, could he play some scales? And when he played them, we heard a new voice—most tiny … a Tinker Bell sound. Miss Peh was singing! We'd never heard her sing before.

As far as we know, that was her first time singing, sitting there on Momma Gung's lap. So I picked her up gently, whispering, "It's OK," and I sat her on top of the piano, holding her so she wouldn't fall. She put both hands on the top of the piano and sat there—feeling the vibrations of the music. She sat there totally awestruck by the music and the vibrations from the piano. When he stopped playing and the vibrations and music stopped, she frowned.

Then we asked the piano man if he could play some ragtime. And when he did, Miss Peh smiled and then grinned, doing her best to clap her hands to the music and, for the first time, moving her feet. Later that day she took two steps, followed by tears. Now, a week later, it's ten steps hanging onto a railing—and then kerplunk, and giggles.

It's Easter. The holiest of all feasts. Our holiest time of the year. It's also Passover. It's Thai New Year—the full moon of the sixth month—the beginning of the monsoons—the beginning of the rice planting season. Soon it will be Miss

Peh's eighth birthday. She marches to a different drumbeat, and her path is not one that most of us would choose, but celebrate life she does. She celebrates with a beauty all her own.

And if you want, next time you hear Handel's *Messiah* or a bit of ragtime—think of us here at the Mercy Centre, think of Miss Peh, this precious and precocious child who has lots of catching up to do. But then again, don't we all?

# Easter at Thai New Year (2006)

Yesterday it felt like everyone in Klong Toey joined us at the Mercy Centre as we celebrated the Thai New Year. Perhaps not totally everybody, but at least several hundred neighbors—mostly old folks and other slum "reputables" and, of course, our kids.

There was great music played on third-hand instruments and dancing in the streets—old-time barn dancing led by the Motorbike Racing Granny, our favorite street vendor, who is now seventy-six. She has a bit of a bum knee, made stiff from kick-starting her stubborn "mini-chopper," a motorbike modified into her mobile coffee cart. Fortunately she had a "wee swallie" or two, or three, from a not so well-hidden flask of amber liquid that loosened her knees and had her stomping up a storm.

In the late morning the monks came for the annual New Year prayers and blessings for our Mercy Centre and to chant the sutras. Our two hundred children were quiet (just for a while), sitting beside an assembly of old and physically challenged folks. And after the prayers everyone made merit and offered the monks a pre-noon meal.

Then the party began. All our children lined up, and one by one they poured lustral water over the cupped hands of the assembled old folks (who represent our children's families) and asked a blessing in return. Our children also gave the old folks parcels of food in a gesture of thanks for the blessing—and, being the kids they are, splashed water everywhere.

Later in the afternoon our kids walked to the nearby slum-friendly Temple by the Bridge, where nine of our boys have become Buddhist novices for the next thirty days, until school holidays are over. Entering the monkhood is a glorious experience for these kids, and the first day is full of ceremonies. The only sad part was at the tonsure ceremony, the point in the day when the parents were supposed to help the monks shave their sons' heads and then float their hair in holy water. Our boys don't have parents, so our Mercy Centre house dads had to take their place.

Our boys become novice monks for many reasons. Most importantly it is a rite of passage in Thailand, much like a confirmation in church or a bar mitzvah at a Jewish synagogue. It is also a way of making merit and showing respect for your parents, for your country and, this year in particular, for His Majesty, the King of Thailand, the longest reigning monarch, in celebration of his sixtieth year on the throne.

Our girls are also having a fabulous time this summer holiday. Besides dancing and music classes, they are also learning to cook, most especially cookies and their favorite Thai dishes. All these activities make them "cool," which is quite important to all children but especially to children, like ours, who have been abandoned.

Almost forgot to mention something. Of the nearly two hundred children living with us, almost every single one of them passed final exams and will move up another grade in school when the new school year begins this May.

Even while our boys join the Buddhist monkhood for a month, we are a Catholic house, and what of that? Yes, we have Holy Week ceremonies and the telling of our sacred truths, but we did all of that last week—because you cannot walk to Jerusalem with Jesus in his sorrow and death and celebrate the festivities of the New Year at the same time. So we did the washing of the feet, and adoration of the Holy Cross and blessings of the baptismal water and fire and earth and air last week. And then this Sunday we celebrate Easter and Jesus rising from the dead. Plus we're going to have a huge Easter egg hunt.

Some might say, "Hey, you can't move feasts around like that!" And they are probably right, but it was either move them or not have them at all. You can't ask Buddhist, Muslim or Christian kids not to party. So we try to give them the best of both worlds.

What a glorious combination of joy and blessings and just plain having a good old time! And our children and old folks and our folks with AIDS and our neighbors and staff and I—we all wish you a Happy New Year and a Happy Easter!

# A Christmas Lullaby (2005)

Did your mom or granny ever sing lullabies? One of our children, who goes by the nickname of Miss Nan, told me she heard someone singing her a Christmas lullaby the other night when it was all quiet in the hospital. A lullaby so sweet, so beautiful, it would make the angels weep.

When she heard it, she awoke, looked around. Only her crippled-up, AIDS-struck, foster-auntie Gung was there. And (heavens to Betsy!) even Miss Nan's pet frog Albert can sing better than Auntie Gung. Everyone in the whole world knows Auntie Gung can't sing. But a lullaby it was that Miss Nan heard.

And who could doubt such a child? Miss Nan, who is only seven and was born with HIV, goes to the hospital a little longer each time now, so she has learned the wisdom of such things. And Auntie Gung stays at her hospital bedside for a week at a time—sometimes two weeks—sleeping at night on a mat on the floor next to Miss Nan's bed.

You see, Auntie Gung, who was born with a congenitally weak spine and has always been frail, can't do much at all. Never could. Wasn't blessed with much on this earth, and what little she had AIDS took away. At first Auntie Gung looked upon sickly Miss Nan as just a sweet but pathetic little girl, but now, with neither of them in the best of health,

Auntie Gung cares for Miss Nan as she would care for her own child. She knows that she was put on this earth, along with (or in spite of) the terrible fatal infection her husband gave her, to receive this special privilege as the surrogate mom for the orphaned Miss Nan. And sometimes when Miss Nan calls out in the night for her mom, Auntie Gung gets up and holds her till she goes back to sleep. Auntie Gung whispers that it's OK to call her momma. And that must be the lullaby Miss Nan hears because for her, Auntie Gung is her Lady Mary, the Virgin Mary—Mother of Jesus in the Christmas legend.

It's Christmas time, a time for special lullabies—the telling of Joseph the Carpenter and Lady Mary and her infant son, the baby Jesus, born in Bethlehem. And it's also time for the silent lullabies Auntie Gung sings to Miss Nan in the quiet of the night.

Our ancient sacred stories date back two thousand years, telling us how Joseph and Mary journeyed for days from Nazareth to the village of Bethlehem, just outside Jerusalem. There in Bethlehem Lady Mary gave birth to Jesus at a local inn, not in a proper room but rather in a stable at the back of the inn as the inn was full. When we recently played a Christmas story to our children in the Mercy Centre, Auntie Gung remarked, "There wouldn't have been room in the inn for Miss Nan and me either, but that's OK. Rooms are not all that important."

And she's right, a stable would do just fine for Miss Nan and Auntie Gung—or even a room in a government hospital, where the nurses talk kindly, just like the shepherds who came to visit the baby Jesus.

And there are other parts in the story that ring true today too—for instance, the part where Joseph the Carpenter has a dream that he must run away with Lady Mary and Jesus from the inn at that moment, in the middle of the night, to flee for their lives out of Bethlehem and start a new life. That's not so different from the moment when Auntie Gung was told that she had a disease, a virus, that her husband would die, that her family and friends would shun her forever after, and that she must leave everything she had known in life and flee to a strange land and start life anew.

And then there's the part about the Magi, the three wise men in the story who traveled from the East, following a star they saw bright in the heavens, to visit the baby Jesus. They had seen the star and searched their own sacred stories and found one about a birth of a child and a star in the East—a star that no storm clouds could ever hide. And maybe they too heard a lullaby in the quiet of the night—so sweet and beautiful it would make the angels weep.

And what of all of this?

Well, Miss Nan and Auntie Gung tell us that sometimes—not often, but sometimes—here in Bangkok town, if you close your eyes real tight and stay very still, you too can see the wise men of the Bible riding on Thai elephants, propelled on the wings of the early morning dawn. And if you keep your eyes closed a bit longer, you can see the wise men riding past your own home, where you and your children can greet them, offering bananas or carrots or apples to their elephants. And then even the worst storm clouds will turn beautiful, and you might be able to catch a glimpse of the star. And then, if you listen intently, you might hear a lullaby—so sweet and beautiful it will make the angels weep.

How can this be? Can it happen? I'm sure of it. Miss Nan and Auntie Gung have told us it's true, and who could doubt them?

And sometimes, right around Christmas, if you listen hard and you still can't hear the lullaby, you too must sing a lullaby softly to your own family—no matter where they are, far away or sitting right beside you.

# Five Ugly Ducklings from the Swamps of Klong Toey: An Easter Letter (2009)

I t starts that way with the Fabulous Five of Klong Toey Kindergarten's Class of 2009–2010—five ugly ducklings. This paddling of ducklings are growing up to be among the most beautiful young men and women on the planet. Maybe not swans, but certainly the greatest of all ducks.

First there's Miss Bhai—her nickname means "the highest branch of the tree touched by the morning sun." Three years ago, when she was two, the Special Branch drug cops did a 3:00 a.m. blast into her momma and papa's Klong Toey shack without knocking, then cuffed and took her folks to the station for possession with intent to sell.

It was especially unpleasant as intent to sell brings with it an industrial-sized prison term. Plus Mom and Pop were small players; they didn't have the ten thousand baht or so cash up front that might have helped them on the way to the station. On top of that, when their agent got word a few minutes later, she wasn't really interested in helping at the police station, as Mom and Pop, in her eyes, were dumb and had been caught before.

Everyone assumed Bhai's granny would come to bundle up the baby and take her home as soon as the uniforms left, since they were locking up Mom and Pop in the Ta Rua (Port Authority) jail, on their way to court and a long stretch in prison. But Granny got distracted. She got the news in the middle of an all-night, all-day card game with some cronies. It was one of those "I won't quit till I win my money back or lose everything" moments. And she let the news slip by her.

Two nights later a thief broke into Mom and Pop's shack. Baby Bhai was lying on the floor, whimpering. The thief was shocked but still stole the rice cooker (probably to save his honor as a thief) plus the drugs the cops didn't find. Then he shouted "Dying baby! Dying baby!" at the top of his lungs and ran into the night. He most probably saved her life. But it took her three months in the communicable diseases hospital to heal her and fatten her up. I forgot to mention, she got AIDS from Mom, who got it from Pop.

That was three years ago. As of late both Mom and Pop are still in prison, getting sicker. Just three weeks ago, Miss Bhai got sick again, but she's over it now. After weeks in hospital she's back with us. "Measles Bhai," as the other members of the Klong Toey Kindergarten Fabulous Five call her.

Almost lost her to the Measles Monster. That, plus the Measles Monster called in an ugly friend—maybe a stray mean orc—who shoved a fistful of pneumonia down her lungs. The doc talked gently but, translated into street talk, he was saying, "This kid's going to the temple in a wooden box." It was five days of touch and go. The odds were bad—two in three, she dies.

She's a tough kid. Beat the odds. She didn't die three years ago, and she didn't die three weeks ago. When she returned to us in a hospital van, the rest of her paddling of the Fabulous Five were waiting. They had skipped kindergarten class when they heard she was coming home—Miss Sim, Miss Dao, Miss Fai and Master Winner.

Bhai insisted that she walk on her own, although she was still pretty wobbly on her pins. They wanted to know about cookies, candy. Did the nurse make you eat all your food? Did she comb your hair nicely? Did you have to take a bath? Did they have school there? Could you watch cartoons? What time did you have to go to sleep? Master Winner wanted to know if anyone had given her a toy car, and the girls wanted to know if she had any new dolls. They had wanted to visit, but she had been quarantined.

Today, if you looked at her, even with her taking the AIDS antivirals twice a day, you wouldn't know. She looks healthy. Eats as much as she can possibly stuff in at each meal, pats her tummy. Doesn't ever want to be hungry again. Last week she completed the school year along with her special paddling of friends, finishing ninth from the top in second-year kindergarten.

Miss Bhai, the number one tough lady of the ugly ducklings, says that classmate five-year-old Miss Sim is almost her favorite girlfriend. Miss Sim, with an armful of burn-scars, is the smallest of the paddling. She actually struck a match and lit her own birthday cake candles last week. We asked her if she wanted to, and she nodded OK—not an easy call for a five-year-old who, just over a year ago, was carried out of a burning shack with singed hair, smoldering clothes and a burned arm, screaming.

Miss Sim's arm has healed. Though it is scarred and certainly not pretty, her arm, hand and finger movements are not impaired. This child fears almost nothing. At five years old she boldly says there are no goblins or monsters under her bed. If there were, she'd whomp 'em just like her granny used to whomp her if she'd make noise when Granny was in a card game. And Miss Sim gets up at night when her best friend Dao knows she's going to wet the bed and is afraid to put her feet on the floor because of the goblins and monsters under there. Sim, whose bed is next to Dao's, checks under Dao's bed to see if "the coast is clear."

# Five Ugly Ducklings from the Swamps of Klong Toey

Miss Dao's been with us two years now. She doesn't have the virus, though her mom did. When Momma was still alive, they moved shacks often. Momma was "the roving kind." The neighbors noticed and often told her off, said she wasn't taking proper care of Dao. Dao's granny told us that finally she herself urged her daughter, "Best you take that baby and go to that foundation. Those people there will at least feed you and Dao. Besides, you're too skinny and sick to keep earning nighttime money anymore." Momma died with us. Miss Dao is now nearly six, and Granny comes to visit when she feels a bit chipper and can hustle bus fare.

Right-hand companion to Dao among the Fabulous Five is Miss Fai—her name means "fluffy cotton like the clouds"—who loves to stand in the rain, letting the raindrops wash her hair and run down her face. She came to us four years ago, a sickly child covered in lice. Back then if you brought Miss Fai near water, even a toilet, she'd go bonkers. Suggest a shower, she'd go hysterical. That's because in the past, her momma, barking mad with each full moon, crazy with the AIDS virus in her brain, would have spells where she would throw water in her daughter's face and then into her own as punishment, screaming the whole time. One night, with another full moon, Momma walked off into the night. Miss Fai is charming, front-toothless, likes to wear her hair short and dresses like a six-year-old fashion model, always neat and clean.

The only boy in this paddling is young Master Winner. He's just like his name—a kid every dad would like as his own son. Wears his Superman costume to kindergarten. Says he wants to live at our farm on the canal with the big boys. Our farm is half an hour's drive out of Bangkok, postage stamp small, but big enough for our street boys to be healed and heal themselves from the scars and horrors of city streets. Our farm boys walk to school, go barefoot, go fishing, grow from boys to men. Master Winner tells us he's ready to join the older boys but doesn't want to go quite yet as his momma couldn't visit him there often.

His momma is gentle, loving, with long black hair down her shoulders. She got the virus from his Western daddy, now disappeared. Or at least so says Momma. She knows his relatives; they blame Momma and won't touch Master Winner with a thirty-foot barge pole. Momma worked in a factory but quit her job for a while, as the daily bus travel was literally killing her. Now she's stronger with the government-sponsored antivirals and has a new job. Got herself a hot water pot and a coffee grinder, and now she sells fresh cups of coffee on the sidewalk in front of a low budget backpackers' hotel. The police there are kind—know she's sick—and they ask no favors. Not even free cups of coffee. And they chase away the bad guys who seek "sidewalk space rent," so Momma survives.

She tells her "truth," and that's OK. She tells what she feels she wants us to know.

She offered us an unbelievable pact. Her idea. I wouldn't have dreamed of such an agreement on my own, nor would our staff. I'm not that smart. Her pact works like this: no matter what, no matter how many days she may eat just rice and fish sauce, no matter how tempting the easy nighttime money might be, no matter how much money she might have to borrow from the money lenders, even at twenty baht a day on one hundred baht, she won't give in. Won't spread the virus—she promises—*if* we care for her youngest son, Master Winner. We gave her our word, and we live and die by our word.

And me, I promised beyond the grave. Heavy stuff. I'm sixty-nine and promised her we'd care for this kid until he grows up, even after I'm dead and gone. The staff said they would keep their word. We will care for Master Winner. So we said, Momma of Master Winner, you try to keep your word, as best as you can. If you goof up, we'll look the other way. Don't worry. We will care for your son. He's part of the Klong Toey Kindergarten Class of 2009–2010. He's a member of the Fabulous Five.

We made our promise, candles and joss sticks in hand, at our Mercy Centre—she in front of a statue of the Buddha and me in front of a statue of the Blessed Virgin Mary.

Momma comes now and then, mostly alone, but sometimes with a boyfriend. When she comes, we ask Master Winner if he wants to help Momma sell fresh cups of coffee over the weekend. Off they go, hand in hand.

This paddling of five of our Klong Toey Kindergarten graduates … they waddle, they quack, they fall down, they get up. They swim without being really taught, and somehow they have found each other in their own beautiful way. Now school's out, and each morning they wake up to try to have as much fun as they possibly can.

They may never turn out to be swans, but fabulous ducks they shall be.

# An Easter Letter (2010)

Holy Week. Easter. Meet you at the Jubilee—with a medium-sized piece of chocolate with only one bite taken out.

It's Friday morning in Holy Week. The day Jesus died. We wear black clothing in sorrow, mourning and respect; leave our jobs for the day, if we can; eat the simplest of foods; take off our shoes to walk barefoot in solemn procession, to show respect to the Holy Cross. Once again, we formally "tell our sacred stories." Relive these events for ourselves and our children. We do this, today in our turn, as our ancestors have done for two thousand years.

How Jesus—after they condemned him, beat him up so badly, force-marched him through the crowds in Jerusalem town out to a lonely hill where they put up three crosses. And there he died in thunder and storm and an eclipse of the sun.

And then his body was taken to a tomb, and three days later, it all changed. He had gone down to Middle Earth, found Adam and Eve and all our ancestors, and told them: "Wake up! Wake up! It's time. We're all going home to heaven." Our long-time-ago great-grandmothers and those of ages beyond went to the tomb—empty—and the Angel said to them, "What are you doing here? He is risen from the dead." They hurried off to tell the men. And the word spread: "Meet you at the Jubilee! We're all going to have a party! Hurry on over!"

And here on earth we still sing joyous songs, light candles, put on happy clothes and flowers in our hair. Maybe like they all said: "Meet you at the Jubilee! Hurry on over!" And our Jubilee is here in Klong Toey with our two hundred kids. Easter eggs and of course chocolate. But back to that in a minute.

You know, it isn't just the Jerusalem of yesterday and getting beat up so badly and dying and three crosses on a lonely hill. It's yesterday and today for each of us. Mostly the road you take to avoid it all is the path that leads to your destiny. But let's not be alone, let's—each of us, side by side—do our own walking through Jerusalem and to the Jubilee.

But the chocolate. Here in the Mercy Centre in the Klong Toey slums of Bangkok, early last evening, I went upstairs to see a five-year-old who was terribly abused. She was running around as usual, but really hanging on to me and one of the house moms, and I started to tear up—silent crying, if you like—and she asked me why I was crying. I didn't say anything, so she gave me a hug and told me to make a funny face, and that would make me better. Then she went over to her locker, took out her "stash" and handed me a piece of chocolate that she'd only taken one bite out of. And it was her last piece. She'd been saving it. And maybe it only takes a medium-sized piece of chocolate candy, with only one bite out of it, to bring us back.

Easter Blessings to each of you! Today is the day the Lord has made.

# Part V

Father Joe's Notepad

# Forty-Five Years as a Priest (2010)

Someone asked me to jot down some words on the celebration of my ordination and first mass—about being a "senior priest." Forty-five years ago—counting from today—as a newly ordained Catholic priest, I said my first mass and gave my first priestly blessings in a wooden church in a small farm town in South Dakota.

It was and still is terribly important to me that I began my official priesthood there, saying my first mass in that rural community, where my Irish and German ancestors homesteaded after the American Civil War. Me, the son of a farmer and a farmer's daughter.

Over the course of these years of my priesthood, it seems that the great rules of evangelization have become clearer. To politely say "good morning" and "good evening" to everyone I meet. To say I am sorry—to apologize when I am wrong, always giving honor to all I meet along the way. To say "thank you" even when it might not seem necessary.

I have been honored and blessed beyond belief in that my religious order, the Redemptorists, sent me to Thailand and then Laos and then, thirty-seven years ago, back to Bangkok to the Slaughterhouse in the slums, to be parish priest for our Catholics who butcher the pigs—where I have been accepted as a true family member and a real part of this beautiful slum community.

My and your stories are not yet finished—the last words have not yet been written, and the final scenes are still open-ended. A songwriter said: "Been doing some hard traveling down the road," and yes, the future is a mystery, but there is hope. There is joy.

# Thai New Year (April 2010): Protests

New Year in Thailand, traditionally, is April 13. The fifth moon of the lunar calendar. So blessings to each of you for the coming year.

May your rice harvest be abundant, with enough to eat in the coming year for you and your children. May your ponds and waterways be abundant with fish. May your water buffalo calve healthy offspring. May your own children be strong and a joy and honor to you. And may your own elders bless you specially. Tomorrow is the day you pour lustral water—perfumed and flowered—over their hands and bow at their feet, thanking them and asking wisdom and courage for the coming year.

I write this from a Bangkok under siege. We do not know what will happen.

Right now, it is a "Don't blink" situation. The prime minister is trying to follow the rule of law and the constitution. The heads of the military and police are ambivalent, trying to keep a foot in both camps. True, there is no real violence—no looting. But the city is semi-paralyzed. And most of all, no one is enjoying the New Year. Normally three million people leave Bangkok and go home to visit their families. This year all of Thailand is in sorrow. As for the present "troubles," we trust and hope to see reason and cooler hearts prevail.

# Forty-Five Years as a Priest (2010)

We of course are safe. Most of our two hundred children here at the Mercy Centre are on school vacation and have gone to the countryside with friends and our own staff for the holidays. The "troubles" are in a small part of the city. I myself am here at the Mercy Centre, "keeping the home fires burning" and also making sure everyone knows that, no matter what, fat old bald-headed Father Joe is here. Not that I can do anything or solve any problem, but everyone feels a bit better and more secure to know I am here.

All for now. Blessings again to you all! We shall survive, but I am worried that difficult days are ahead for our beloved Bangkok and all of Thailand.

# One Month after the Protests (2010)

I write to you in early June, following the "Burning of Bangkok"—demonstrations and protests that hobbled our fair city for two months, pouring lethal acid into the very soul of the land, an acid that spread into every Bangkok shantytown and far beyond.

Here in Klong Toey our children at the Mercy Centre played "make-up games" in the streets, as did the children behind the barricades, but children do that everywhere. We remain unscathed physically. Emotionally the wounds and scars run raw and deep, and we pray for peace, justice and the meekness of wisdom.

During the height of the troubles there were public notices on TV and radio stations stating that our Mercy Centre was a safe haven for all children and needy adults. Also our older children joined with our slum neighbors, keeping night watch against arson and mayhem.

Life went on, trembling, fearful and poorer than before. Our neighbors lost income during and after the protests that was lost forever. Moms and dads couldn't work to feed their families, pay their debts and keep their kids going to school.

Where does all this leave the Mercy Centre? The answer is that we're here among our neighbors, with all our children—forever, keeping the home fires burning. If it should ever come (as it has and will) that there is not enough rice in our common rice bowl, we adults will cut back and make sure the children have enough. As more children come to us, if we don't have enough beds, we can put mats on the floor. If shoes wear out, we can put new heels and soles on them, and when school uniforms wear thin, from wear and tear and too many washings, we'll patch them. That's what we've always done anyway and continue to do to this day. Hand-me-downs certainly fit just as well as new clothes, sometimes even better.

If we are careful, there is always just enough. But if any of you good folks reading this have anything left over, please do share it with our kids. I do know that all of you, as part of our family, are "always there for us," and we shall never ask unless our need is dire or the situation critical.

Finally. Above I spoke of the "meekness of wisdom." Please pray that these words become the watchwords for our slums and all of Thailand.

# The Rights of the Child

To be here today, of course I had to ask permission from all our children in our Janusz Korczak School in the Klong Toey slums of Bangkok, especially the ones in their early teens, both boys and girls, because in many ways they are more fragile and vulnerable, and bruise more easily than the smallest and youngest. The younger ones hurt for the moment; the older ones hurt for a lifetime.

I come before you from Bangkok with a nearly impossible task—to imagine that Dr. Janusz Korczak is sitting here in the front row, listening to what all of us are saying. And of course he is here in spirit.

I am here to give you a message from our children, the Janusz Korczak children of the Klong Toey slums of Bangkok. And if my message rings true and clear—and you can hear the voices of our children—then I know Dr. Janusz approves, and more important, our children approve. And if our children approve, then the children of the whole world approve.

Our children, formerly street kids, used and abused throwaways who live with us as family, have several messages. First, they wish to say, "We the Janusz Korczak

223

children of Klong Toey are OK. Not perfect. Not a hundred percent, but doing OK—and we hope that you are OK." And from the younger ones, "Do you know how to play rock-paper-scissors, and how many times can you skip rope without missing a step?" And so the children ask you, do your children do this?

I do not come bringing a magical formula for protecting children—only a message from our children. But maybe it is magic.

The essence of our children's message is that every child has an absolute right to protection from each and every adult they meet. All children—every single one—when they see any adult anywhere—on the street, in school, especially at home—can look at that adult and know they will be protected. Loved. Looked after. No matter what. That they will not be harmed. They are safe. That's why I am here today, to bring you this message from the Janusz Korczak Children of Bangkok.

I have fulfilled my part of my bargain with the children, and now I hope that you have a message for me to take back to our kids in Bangkok. They will feel honored if you can send them your kind wishes. And if you ever pass through Bangkok, better still, please visit our Mercy Centre. Our children insist. We have two hundred kids who live with us at our Mercy Centre in Klong Toey, including our Janusz Korczak kids in our homes and our school. But allow me to explain …

At our Mercy Centre, Janusz Korczak is not just about a school building we named in his honor. Nor is Korczak just about the street children who attend this school, children who have no other place to go to learn to read and write and make friends. Korczak is about much more than a school that opens each day, Monday through Friday, from eight in the morning until three-thirty in the afternoon.

Janusz Korcak is a part of every child we meet on the streets, twenty-four hours every day. He is a part of everything in the lives of these children—he is the way these children live on the streets and in school, the way they play and grow up, mature and lead lives raising their own families.

We teach and feed another three thousand Janusz Korczak kindergarten kids each day in thirty slums in Bangkok, as well as almost a thousand sea gypsy kids down in the middle-south of Thailand. Plus seventy kids with HIV in Bangkok who live with their parents and grannies in shacks. Plus hundreds more kids, rag-pickers' kids, kids living under bridges. They are all our Korczak children.

We have one important rule that we ask each of our Korczak children to follow: if they see a poor kid in their neighborhood who is not going to school, they *must* tell us and let us help. We need to teach our children that the first rule of caring for themselves is to care for others. That is our one hard-and-fast rule, the only one we ask of our children.

But what are their rules? What rules do Bangkok's poorest children live and play by to survive? Here are the rules we've distilled from forty years of listening to them, being guided by them. These children are our teachers in the world of human rights.

First, the primary rule of living on the streets—this is what the experienced street children tell the new ones on their first day on the street: **Find an adult you can trust. You cannot make it on your own.** You might not find one. It's not that easy. But your problems are too big to handle by yourself. Besides, if you are alone and something happens … there will not be anyone to tell your granny and then no one to pray for you at the temple or at the church or mosque.

Please allow me to digress. A granny's rights, at least in our Klong Toey slum, are equally important in understanding children's rights. Their rights are inextricably bound together as it is often the granny who is raising the child. They live together and, to put it bluntly, keep each other alive.

Grannies' rights include:

**The right to chew betel nut.** This includes the right to live and to teach her traditions and folkways to her grandkids.

**The right to own a cat, a dog and a python snake under the shack to get the rats**

**The right to fair play from the police**

**The right to fair play from the schoolteachers who teach their grandchildren**

**The right to a bowl of rice**—that is, to eat regularly, most of the time

As for the street kids, their rights include:

**The right to "own" a puppy dog, or at least have one around, and to clean up after its poop, feed it and care for it.**

All children, even street children, need to feel responsible for someone or something. And as I've already mentioned, a street kid is usually responsible for his granny who raised him in the shack.

More children's rights:

**The right to be listened to, talked to and heard out**

**The right not to be given up on ... always to have another chance**

**The right to be stubborn.** Usually kids will not change their minds, and that's OK.

**The right to a better education—to make choices**

Every slum kid knows how to count by the time he's three or four. They count money, count cards, count the number of times they skip a rope. There are future poets, scholars, professors, judges and leaders of industries and the arts among the kids we meet on the street. They just need a safe place to live and the chance to go to school.

We at our Mercy Centre and everywhere in the world must take another look at the way we see children and re-examine it, and realize the honor and privilege of having children trust you, especially abused and abandoned kids, and what a great honor it is to allow them to be our teachers.

More rights:

**The right to make mistakes and to be forgiven for them**

**The right to get into fights and resolve conflicts according to children's rules, not adult rules**

**The right to a daddy who comes home most nights, and not drunk**

**The right to a momma who lives with Daddy in a home where neither Momma nor Granny get beat up, physically or verbally, by Daddy**

**The right to Daddy's salary, so he gives it to Momma or Granny to buy food without spending it all on booze and cigarettes**

**The right *not* to see men or boys or cops beating up girls and women, calling them horrible names that are not true ... or even if they are true**

**The right to go to school with rice in your tummy**

**The right to look nice—to have your hair combed and to be bathed with clean water, not smelly canal water from Bangkok's *klongs*—which makes all the other kids and, worst of all, the teachers, tell you that you stink**

**The right to wash your clothes ... and to have clothes to wash**

**The right to have someone love you and hold you**

**The right to know and understand what you can and cannot do**

**The right to make everyday choices—to choose your own school bag and everyday things that are meaningful perhaps only to you**

Finally, most importantly …

**The right to have as much fun as you can every day**

We borrow the name Janusz Korczak for our school because, well, to put it in modern language: "He was cool. So cool that he didn't even have to try to be cool." He knew what kids are about. (And lots of big dumb adult folks, who forgot everything their mommas ever taught them, wanted to change the rules.)

Our Korczak kids wake up early in the morning and say, "I'm going to have as much fun as I possibly can all day today. Might have to go to school. That's OK. I shall make that fun too."

So … back to our children and the deal I made with them before I left for this conference. I had to bribe them with ice cream. Of course, we all know bribes are wrong, but ice cream? That's different!

"*Why* are you going?" they asked. And most of all they wanted to know, "Will you come back? Will you return to Mercy? We have been abandoned before. We kind of trust you … but you can never be sure about adults. They break their word often, especially when they promise to do something for us or say they will give us something."

My brothers and sisters—relatives, cousins, aunts and uncles, members of our Janusz Korczak Family … I, one of your relatives, come before you from Bangkok to speak in the name of our children who live with us here at the Mercy Centre in Klong Toey and of our teachers and kids of our Janusz Korczak School of Southeast Asia. Thus it is an honor for me to be here. An honor that the children allowed me to come. An honor that you have asked me to come. It is also a fearsome, an awesome, responsibility for me—a Western-born, Irish-American Catholic priest living forty years in Bangkok, Thailand—to speak in the name of Thai children.

So how did I convince the children? Of course I told them the truth—that I wanted to talk about the Rights of the Child. And some of the older ones said, "By the way, we have been wanting to talk to you about the Rights of the Child."

"And what are these rights?" I asked them.

They said, "We have the right to go to school," and remarked that it is what they thought Headmaster Janusz Korczak would say too. I prefer to name him Headmaster, as that is the way our children see him. And, really, if that's how our children wish to respect him, what else matters?

Our kids told me they wish to follow Headmaster Korczak's principles of going to school, but also to follow the rules on the streets and in the slums. This is quite difficult because they seem to be two distinctly different sets of rules. Can our children follow street-survival rules and still go to school? Are they contradictory? *Almost*. So the child and the teacher and all of us have to change. We have to listen.

We try to make everyone listen and have even translated into Thai Korczak's Rights of the Child, as listed at the end of B.J. Lifton's wonderful biography, and we give them to every policeman and judge and lawyer we meet when we defend children involved in the judicial system—that is, in over eighty local police stations and all the children's courts in Bangkok.

Our children know and want to believe in the rights of the child. Except that many of them don't, or aren't able to, because a lot of bad teachers have taught them otherwise, just as they have been taught to feel hate and prejudice.

So what we do is this. We dress up in doctoral robes and our children wear caps and gowns at our Mercy Kindergarten graduation day. And we tell them, go to school. *Go to school.*

Momma plays cards, loses all the money … go to school.

Dad drinks, beats up on Momma … go to school.

It's raining and your shack is flooded … go to school.

It's a sunny beautiful day … go to school.

No shoes to wear … go to school.

No breakfast, no porridge, there's a deep hunger in your belly … go to school.

No matter what … *go to school!*

It's your right. It's every poor kid's right. And it's the only chance in life you'll ever get.

Photo by Yoonki Kim

Father Joe Maier, C.Ss.R. has ministered to the poor in Bangkok's slums for over 40 years. As the Parish Priest of the Catholic community, he has lived alongside the poor residents around the city's main slaughterhouse in Klong Toey slums—which is how he became known as "The Slaughterhouse Priest." Fr. Joe co-founded the Human Development Foundation - Mercy Centre, a community-based organization dedicated to strengthening the poorest slum communities of all religions and protecting and educating their most vulnerable children.

Pictured above: Fr. Joe dons his doctoral robes once a year and presents a certificate to every graduating student of the Mercy Centre kindergartens, which have produced over 40,000 graduates to date. For more information and how you can help, please visit: www.mercycentre.org.

# Human Development Foundation – Mercy Centre
## The History

The Human Development Foundation began on an early morning in 1973, as it has every day since, with a daily walk in the slum neighborhoods. Father Joe and Sister Maria saying good morning to all their neighbors. How are you today? Do you have any food for breakfast? Is there anything we can do to help? Fr. Joe was the Parish Priest for the Catholics who butchered the pigs. The parishioners lived and worked in the slaughterhouse of Klong Toey, Bangkok's largest slum community. Sr. Maria came daily from her Convent and began teaching Catechism to the Catholic children. She actually taught the children where they played… in a seldom-used holding pen for pigs.

In 1973 Slaughter House kids did not go to school, and the few who did failed dismally and dropped out. The one or two schools available begrudgingly took them in. Teachers singled them out as what not to be.

Telling anyone "I'm from the Slaughter House" marked you like an ugly tattoo—branded you forever. You couldn't go to school. Couldn't get a real job. Butchering pigs, washing entrails, frying down pork fat into lard… these were the choices available.

Sr. Maria and Fr. Joe turned a slum shack into a one-baht-per-day preschool for every child in the Slaughter House, children of all religions. No child was turned away. Thus (without saying so or calling itself anything) began The Human Development Foundation. Now, today in 2012, there are twenty-two Mercy Kindergartens with over 2,500 slum children going to school. Alumni of the first Slaughter House kindergarten are teachers, executive secretaries, nurses, two lawyers, taxi drivers, and butchers. Many are now married with their own children attending proper schools. Dead-end, throw-away slaughter house kids no longer.

For more information about Mercy Centre and to find out how you can help, please visit www.mercycentre.org. For inquiries, email info@mercycentre.org.